Conversations With My Mother
Reflections on the Death of a Parent

Conversations With My Mother
Reflections on the Death of a Parent

by

Melville Gary Finkelstein

1stBooks – rev. 5/1/00

ABOUT THE BOOK

Conversations With My Mother is Melville's emotional journey of coming to terms with his mother's death. It's an inspirational story of how life continues on in the face of tragedy. The book consists of daily conversations created from Melville's thoughts and feelings.

The book deals with Melville's feelings of loss, grief and despair. It speaks of his feelings of helplessness and anger when his mother became sick, and the author describes his feelings of inadequacy because there was nothing he could do to help her. He blamed himself for not having the foresight to know that something was "very wrong," as his mother had said. It also talks about his anger toward the doctors. Why didn't *they* know more?

Conversations. . . also describes his mother's eulogy and burial, the cleaning out of her apartment and how one rises to the occasion to deal with the legal considerations and other responsibilities that take place after a parent dies.

Melville, falling into the depths of depression, is shocked back into reality by an unforeseen event. He comes to terms with his mother's death and begins to concentrate on living life again. The experience has made him realize the relationship between life, time, and a person's dreams.

This book is a tribute that can be related to anybody's mother. It shows a mother's strong characteristics, how she survives in the face of tragedy, loss and pain, and how she simply wants to love and be good to her family. A mother's humbleness makes her children want to be with her and near her. The author recognizes that a mother possesses a great knowledge of the human condition and that it's a mother's spirit and solid foundation that make us proud of her.

In Loving Memory
of my Parents,
Yetta and Jack

ACKNOWLEDGMENTS

I want to thank Othello Anzolut for all the fatherly advice I received over the years, and who, with my wife, Kay, had the idea and encouraged me to put these conversations into book form. I also want to thank my family and friends who are the subject matter of these conversations. A special thanks to my wife, Kay, for asking me out on our first date. I finally have to thank my mother. I hope this tribute makes her proud. Thank you, Mel Finkelstein, NYC 1998

Author's Note: Some names were changed to preserve confidentiality.

PREFACE

August 14, 1996

It's very hard for me to accept my mother's death. I suppose it's hard for anybody to accept the death of a parent. It just didn't seem that it was time for my mother to die. She seemed so alert and aware. She wasn't sick, except for having arthritis and typical old age ailments. She never complained about a chest pain. Even in the hospital when she was sick she said she didn't have any chest pains. She couldn't believe that she was so sick. She even asked me if I believed it. I told her I didn't, but when we were waiting to go down to the operating room I saw this look of terror on her face. She was frightened and scared (she wrote that on the pad for me to read because the tube down her throat prevented her from speaking). I wonder if she knew what the outcome would be. I know the thought that she might not survive was on her mind because when Dora, my brother Alan's mother-in-law, was visiting in the hospital and she told my mother that next year they would go to Las Vegas, my mother pointed up to the sky.

Just as the rabbi tore my shirt over my heart to signify that we were in mourning, my heart has another permanent scar which will be there until I die. I'm sorry I saw her in what seemed to be so much discomfort, although the doctor told me she wasn't suffering. It was distressing to see my mother like that. I hope she is with my father again, reunited after thirty-two years. I have to accept the fact that she is now at peace and hope her death has not ended communication with her. I loved her and if she could hear me, she would know it.

August 15, 1996 5:00 P.M.

Hi Ma,

It's about this time of the day when I would call you and ask you how you are and you would usually say "pretty good." You would also tell me you went down into the park and sat and talked with some people. You always said you saw Dora and Lou and that it was a beautiful day. I miss hearing that. When I would call, you would tell me about Alan, that you spoke to him in the morning, and tell me if Bert called during the day. You would tell me about the news you saw on TV, how the world had changed and you didn't understand it. We would talk about the family and many other things. I wonder what you would say today if you knew that I was meeting Alan tonight and we were going to split up your jewelry. Bert can't make it. Fortunately, your biggest fear, that Alan and Bert would not be friends, was unfounded; things are fine between them.

We are all so occupied with financial matters that it seems to take precedence in our lives. By the way, you were right when you said you know your children count your money. I did it also. But truly Ma, I didn't want the money, and was not ready to move into your apartment. I hope you believe that.

I write these letters because it helps me communicate with you. I hope you are at peace. I also hope that I find this out someday. It will make me feel better. I love you, Ma, and will always miss you, no matter how much time goes by. Love, Mel.

Monday, August 19, 1996 3:25 P.M.

Hi Ma,

I went up to your house yesterday. It was painful for me. I cried. I stood and looked at the bed where you were sitting when we took you to the hospital and I cried. I'm having a hard time of it. To realize that you're not here any more is so difficult. I keep thinking how I want it not to be. But, I know, that this is the way it is. You have passed away, and I can't communicate with you anymore. I can only write these thoughts and hope that you somehow hear what I am saying. I never thought you were going to die. I figured the operation would go well and you would be fine, but the heart attack was too severe and your heart was badly damaged. I wonder if you knew what your chances were. You never regained consciousness after the operation. I don't know if you knew we were there, but I hope that you did. We stayed by your side. The painful part of it was, we could not help you. Your heart was just not strong enough to keep your body alive. I'm sorry that we didn't realize that something was wrong all these months that you were complaining. The constant belching caused you much discomfort and must have been a sign of something being very wrong, just as you said. Why the doctors could not see that your arteries were clogged . . . who knows. When I saw you in the hospital, after the operation, it appeared to me that you were in a lot of pain, and this was very distressing to me. However, the doctors assured me that you were not in any pain. I could only pray that they were right.

I hope I can move into your house and live there. Not that I'm afraid . . . I know that you would never do anything to hurt me. I should be ashamed to even think that. There are good spirits in the house, Dad's, yours and

2

Baba's. You all watched out for me and I hope you continue to do so. I guess I'm just not used to your not being there and I'm not really ready to move in. I feel very uncomfortable, although I know I shouldn't be; I know you wanted me to have the apartment, and I feel that keeping it will keep you close to me. I love you, Ma, and I will talk to you later. Love, Mel.

Tuesday, August 20, 1996 5:20 P.M.

An interfering thought

Hi Ma,

I feel nervous today. All these crazy thoughts are going through my head. I said to myself today, I'm sad that you died; I'm glad that you died. That's weird. How can I think that? How can I be glad? I'm crying my eyes out over this . . . I don't understand where this thought has come from. It has no meaning. It's an interfering thought. I love you, and I think I showed it beyond a shadow of a doubt. I'm sorry to have even had that thought. I'm still in shock over your death. It was completely unexpected. I surely thought you would survive the operation and recover. But what if you did survive the operation and you weren't the same person anymore? What if there were some permanent damage done, and you couldn't enjoy life anymore? Maybe that's where this thought comes from.

Business is pretty good. Is it wrong of me to talk of going on vacation? You died three weeks ago. I'm confused. I don't know what's right and what's wrong.

Wednesday, August 21, 1996 8:55 A.M.

Hi Ma,

I met one of our neighbors, Ethel Mark, on the bus this morning. You remember Ethel, Ma, she was my grade school teacher. Since I started going to the synagogue to say Kaddish, we've become good friends. She and her husband, Saul, are very involved with the synagogue. Anyway, Ethel said you were watching over me. I really believe that. I'm sorry for those things that I thought about yesterday. I didn't mean to think that. I don't know why I did. I won't think about that anymore. I'm really very sad and upset about your death. Maybe the bad thought comes from a place of anger. Maybe it doesn't come from anywhere. I know you loved me. I remember when I was in the hospital for one night when I first got multiple sclerosis, and when I came home the next day, you came running in from the kitchen and hugged and kissed me. You were really happy to see me. It was truly a mother's love. It makes me cry to think about that today.

Jarett came over last night to get his yerushah (inheritance). I asked him if he was happy and he said a nice thing, "I'm not happy that I got it." Well Ma, I have to go to work now. I will speak to you later.

Wednesday, August 21, 1996 5:40 P.M.

Hi Ma,

I booked a Caribbean cruise for February. I'm going with Alan and Sharon and people from Sharon's office. It makes me think about the Bermuda cruise we were all going to take in August 1997. A lot of people were ready to go with us and we were going to have one big party!

4

You were going to bunk with Dora, Alan and Sharon were coming, so were Lenny and Michele, even Kay's parents, Josie and Bob, and her sister, Johanna, were going to come. Kay's friends, Mary Ann and Lorraine were ready, too! You said you would love to go and were really looking forward to it. Unfortunately, that won't happen. I can hear you saying, "It wasn't meant to be." I remember you always said, "You can't tell God what you want; He doesn't ask any questions; He does what He wants." Well, Ma, that's what happened here. God didn't ask me or anybody . . . He just took you. We are supposed to be happy about this because it's God's will . . . but I tell you, it's hard for me to accept this and not to ask why. Why did He have to put you through the mental anguish and hardship of the operation? He should have made it easy for you. You deserved that. But who am I to question? What happened, happened, and we can't go back now. I love you, Ma, and you will always be with me. Love, Mel.

Thursday, August 22, 1996 5:17 P.M.

Hi Ma,

It's starting to set in that you're no longer with us. I must say, I still have my moments of disbelief, such as right now. When I think about it, it makes me a little weak in the knees. That I was speaking to you a few weeks ago, and I can't speak to you now, is unbelievable to me. The reality of having lost you has really shaken me, but I am resilient. I will bounce back. I don't think you would want it any other way. I have to go meet Kay now, so I'm going to cut it short. I love you, Ma.

Friday, August 23, 1996 10:50 A.M.

Hi Ma,

It's slow this week in the office, so I'm taking this opportunity to talk to you. Yes, there is some business, but it's summer, so it's really not what it should be. I never got to tell you about our trip to Alaska. You saw a few photos, but I really didn't share the experience with you and that makes me sad. At least I talked to you when I was traveling, calling you at each stop we made. When I spoke to you Friday night, July 19, you sounded so alert and strong. I never expected that you would be sick when we came home. Taking you out of the house to the hospital and you saying, "I hope I see my house again," is one of those things I will never forget. You knew, based on experience with others, that when you go to the hospital at this "stage of the game," you don't make it back. You just knew, Ma. I have to go now. I'll speak to you later. Love, Mel.

Friday, August 23, 1996 3:30 P.M.

Hi Ma,

I'm sitting here thinking about the eulogy. Everybody thought the rabbi was wonderful. The rabbi based his eulogy on what I had told him. I spoke to him for about 15 - 30 minutes and told him about you. I remember starting at the point when Dad died. I had said that instead of letting your family down, you looked responsibility squarely in the face. You knew you had to earn a living. I was twelve years old and you didn't want to let me down. You didn't! You brought me up and dealt with not only your emotional feelings but also with the emotional problems I was having. Thinking back, it must've been

6

distressing for you to see me in so much pain because there was nothing you could do to help. I would say that's the same feeling I had seeing you in the hospital. I told the rabbi you went to work and became a supervising clerk in the welfare department until you retired. I told him that Baba was also living with us and you had a responsibility to take care of her. I told him how kind you were. An example I gave him was, once we had groceries delivered to the house by a young kid. It was summer and he was wearing a sweatshirt and you said to him, "Would you like two blue polo shirts?" He said yes, and you gave them to him. Then you said, "Why don't you put one of them on now, it's so hot."

I told the rabbi how your life before Dad died was not an easy one . . . coming through the Depression and how sometimes Dad didn't work and money was tight. I told him about how when I got sick with the multiple sclerosis you would have done anything to help me, such as buying me that special pillow. I needed the pillow to keep my head raised so I wouldn't get dizzy. I don't remember exactly what else I told him, but he said to me, "It seems like your mother was dedicated to her family and their well-being was a priority after your father died." He was right. That's exactly what you were: dedicated.

In the eulogy he compared you to a tree: unwavering and strong. And your family found comfort being in the shadow of that tree. They felt safe. This was very true, Ma. You took care of everybody and I told you many times that you should be proud of yourself.

The rabbi also said it was not your destiny to live the last thirty-two years with Dad. But that didn't stop you from taking on the responsibility you saw as yours. It's unfortunate that you were cheated out of those years. We even discussed that on occasion. But you said, and I repeat, "God doesn't ask; He just does."

I told him that you were opinionated and he said that in the eulogy. He said you had four grandchildren, Jason, Stacey, Jarett and Lisa. People who came to the chapel said it was like the rabbi knew you personally. I told him how we played Mah Jongg. I told you were fun to be with, that we enjoyed your company. Even how you kibitzed in the hospital when they had you on the oxygen and Kay said you're getting the royal treatment and you said, "The royal treatment I need!?"

After the rabbi's eulogy, Alan got up and spoke and said some nice things about your brother, Ben, and Dora and Kay and me. We were all touched by his words, and Ma, if you could only have heard it, you would've been crying, too. It's not everyone who gets to hear their own eulogy, but I have a copy of Alan's, so here it is:

"Today is a day of sadness and reflection. Those who knew our mother appreciated her soft-spoken manner and easy-going wit. Her motto was, 'If it's good for you, it's good for me.' If she were here today, she might have said, 'It's a beautiful day out. Go have fun, don't fuss over me.' That's just the kind of lady Mama was.

"Family always came first with Mom. Her main concern was the health and happiness of her children and their families. Each of us spoke to her daily and her first thoughts were always of her grandchildren. She took tremendous pride in their accomplishments.

"My Mom had a special affection for her brothers, Lou and Ben. She loved them very much and placed tremendous value on Ben's judgment. He was her brother, friend and confidant.

"To my mother-in-law, Dora, my heartfelt thanks. You were like a sister to our mother over the past year. Mom always knew she could count on you for anything and you never disappointed her.

"Bert and I want to give a very special thanks to Mel and Kay, who gave of themselves unhesitatingly to ensure that Mom was well and happy. No one could ask for more caring children and they hold a very special place in Mom's heart.

"I would like to thank all of you for your support and love through this difficult time. I know we'll all miss her."

Jason also got up and spoke some nice words.

Ma, you were my best friend and a wonderful person and people should look upon you as an example of how to live. Ma, I love you and miss you. Mel.

Monday, August 26, 1996 4:30 P.M.

Hi Ma,
I would usually see you over the weekend, but unfortunately, I can't anymore. I just spoke to your brother, Ben. He said he misses talking to you. Today is Monday, and this would be the day he would call you. He can't believe what happened to you. But we all have to realize what has occurred and get on with our lives.

I was in your house yesterday going through all your clothes. I think if you saw what you had you would laugh. You had at least: seventy-three housecoats; fifty-three skirts; ninety-two blouses; forty-two pairs of shoes (including sneakers) and a huge variety of coats, sweaters, and other accessories. Ma, you even had Baba's fur stole from a million years ago! You had a lot of clothes. And this is not to mention the food stuff (like the ten quarts of cooking oil) and paper goods. I know you didn't have any idea of all the stuff you had in the back of those cabinets and closets.

We split the "goodies" among Bert, me, Dora and Josie. You had enough tomato sauce for a year. You must've had fifteen gallons of detergent. I think every time it was on sale you bought it. It was hysterical seeing all you had in the house — you were well prepared for the next catastrophe, whatever it may have been, but it was also hard rummaging through your belongings, knowing that you were in the house just a few weeks ago. It's difficult to walk in the house and know you're not there. I would also call out "Ma" so you would know it was me and I wouldn't scare you. I'm going to Shul on Friday and Saturday to say Kaddish for you. It's not only what I'm supposed to do for you, it also helps me get through this tough time.

I keep thinking back, if only I was able to know something was wrong months before . . . maybe they could've done the bypass sooner and you could've lived longer. I can kick myself for not knowing. I feel I should've been smarter, but I wasn't. I don't know if I could've been. When I called Steve, the son of your friend Ruth, to tell him what happened to you, he said, "You can't look back." Ruth had a stroke and survived, but Steve had to make some decisions, such as not resuscitating her. He said, "You make these decisions and you can't look back." The doctors are the ones that should've figured out that something was wrong. Well, Ma, I'll talk to you more tomorrow. I love you and hope you are resting in peace. Mel.

Tuesday, August 27, 1996 4:40 P.M.

Hi Ma,

Business is pretty good this week, but I have to make an effort to do more because we're going to need a lot of money to fix up the apartment. As a matter of fact, we're looking into getting a mortgage. Also, the rent is going to be higher. Well, what are you going to do? As I said before, I wasn't ready to move into your apartment. I have to now. I have no choice. I know you wanted me to have it. There's a void in my life without you here. I miss talking to you. I miss you. Love, Mel.

Wednesday, August 28, 1996 10:00 A.M.

Hi Ma,

I spoke to Bert yesterday morning. He was telling me he has trouble sleeping at night because he is thinking about you. He also told me Alan called him. I think you would be happy about that.

I had trouble sleeping last night, too. What keeps going through my head are different scenarios of what could've happened with the outcome always being that you survived. But then reality sets in and I realize you're not here and it makes me feel sad.

My leg and arm are bothering me. I wonder if it's just a reaction to your death or the MS is acting up. Maybe my being so upset just set off something in relation to the MS. We'll see what happens. I have an appointment with a new doctor on September 16. His name is Dr. Stein.

Josie and Bob are going to take your living room furniture. The bedroom furniture may be taken by Kay's nephew Jaime and his fiancée, Denise. They will be getting married soon. I don't know what to do with the pots and pans. There's a lot of work that has to be done. We'll take our time and do it systematically until we get everything out and have the kitchen and bathroom redone and move in. I will talk to you later. Please be in peace. Love, Mel.

Thursday, August 29, 1996 11:00 A.M.

Hi Ma,
I had a photo of you cropped and enlarged today. It looks beautiful. I'm going to put it in a place in the house where we know you will be watching over us. I paid for the photos out of your account, but as Kay said this morning it's hard to get it out of our heads that it's not your money anymore. Every time I read the will (the part that you wrote) it makes me cry. This is what you wrote:

Dear Alan, Bert and Mel,

I will try to divide everything to the best of my ability, but when it comes to family heirlooms such division is impossible. If you want to change with one another, that is up to you.

12

What I am going to do now is the hardest part, it hurts me, but I have to do this in order to avoid arguments and friction between all of you.

I want only my sons, not their wives, to be involved, so I am sure all will be fine.

If I give one thing, and you want to change with each other, it is up to you.

I will try to cover everything that I have and can remember.

I want my jewelry and other heirlooms to be kept in the family. They belong to the family and you are only keeping them for the next generation.

Please don't throw out my baby pictures, wedding pictures, daddy's picture and my family pictures.

Alan, take your family pictures and Bar Mitzvah album. Bert, take your family pictures and Bar Mitzvah movies. Mel, take the pictures, Bar Mitzvah pictures. Alan, any pictures left, put them in your attic.

Paintings in living room, take and share whatever you want. Small picture over club chair, don't sell or give away. Keep it, the frame is gold leaf.

Also, let Mel take the small picture over the wing chair and the other one (a few houses, bridge and water under the bridge framed in gold). Also, give him my wedding band and Baba's band, for sentimental reasons.

Before dividing the money, pay all my bills. Put plaque in Shul near daddy's. Get tombstone to match daddy's and put brass bed and stones. If you can't say Kaddish hire one.

I think I covered everything . . . if not, do what you think best.

13

Please remain friends all your lives, no matter if you ever disagree. Nothing is so important as remaining good friends, besides being brothers.

I hope that what I did was right and you understand what I mean.

I love you all very much, my three sons, Alan, Bert and Mel . . .

Your loving mother.

It's been a month since you died. Time has gone by very fast. I guess I'm over the initial shock of it, but I must say I'm very sad that you're not here with me anymore. I was wondering if the next thirty-two years will go by as fast as the last thirty-two. I'm referring to the thirty-two years since Dad died in 1964. I don't know where those years went, but if I live the next thirty-two years I will be seventy-six years old. It probably is going to fly by. I'm trying to deal with it on some level somewhere and accept the fact that you died. Does a person ever get over it? I guess I'll accept it at some point but never get over it. I have to go. I'll speak to you later.

Friday, August 30, 1996 3:00 P.M.

Hi Ma,

I went to the co-op office today to get a move in-move out pass and while I was there I straightened out the paperwork for your apartment to make everything legal. I'm doing this to reassure myself that I get your apartment and to also be able to vote for reconstitution. The cooperators will be voting within the next couple of months on whether or not to reconstitute our housing development. Reconstitution is a plan for converting the housing development from a government-regulated cooperative to a completely private cooperative. One result of this conversion will be that the value of the apartments will be increased. I am hoping that it will pass and that I'll be able to sell my apartment and use the proceeds to pay Alan and Bert for their share of your apartment so I'll have your apartment free and clear. I'm doing these things without even thinking about you. When I think about you, it makes it hard for me to make these moves. But, I'm handling it like a business deal and not letting my emotions get in the way. I don't want to feel guilty that I'm taking your apartment away from you. It's ridiculous! Why should I feel guilty? You wanted me to have the apartment! You loved me and wanted only for me to be happy. Having the two-bedroom apartment will make me happy, just as long as you always know I wasn't really ready to get it yet. I didn't need it or want it at this point in my life. But now I have no choice. It hurts me to look at your photo and realize that you're not here with me, but this is reality. The pain will lessen over time, but the scar of your loss will always be there. I don't know what else to say about it except that I am very sad. It's going to take time for me to bounce back. I'm going to call Alan now, so I'll speak to you later.

Tuesday, September 3, 1996 1:00 P.M.

Hi Ma,

It's been a long weekend. Mary Ann, Kay and I worked on cleaning out your house the whole weekend. It was a lot of work, but we're almost finished. Kay's nephew Jaime is getting married and wants the furniture so he is coming over the weekend to take both bedroom sets. Josie and Bob are taking the living room set, Kay's sister, Johanna, is going to take the breakfront, and Kay's niece

JoAnn and her husband, Randy, are going to take some of your pictures. So all the furniture is going to people who knew you and will appreciate it. You had 200 hanks of wool which I gave to Ethel Mark as a donation for a Jewish organization that she belongs to. She said that a lot of members are women your age who knit. I also gave her your handbags.

What I would give to talk to you one more time. I never thought when I said good-bye to you at the operating room door that it would be the last good-bye. I feel numb. It's going to take a long time for me to get over this. I feel nervous, uncomfortable, weak, listless and I'm doing things just out of habit and not concentrating on them. I feel like I'm somewhere else. I just don't want to get sick myself. I'll speak to you later. Mel.

Tuesday, September 3, 1996, 5:30 P.M.

Hi Ma,

Rosh Hashanah is coming in a couple of weeks and Alan invited Bert, Gail and her father to the house for the holiday. I hope it makes you happy because it makes me happy. I keep thinking of you the last day we were able to talk to each other. You were holding my hand and moving your thumb up and down against my thumb. It seems that you were thinking about what was going to happen. It reminds me of when I saw Dad sitting in front of the kitchen window the night before he died. He knew he was sick and he was looking out the window wondering and thinking about what was going to happen. It hurts me to think about that, and to think about you lying in the coffin in the grave. I'm sure those thoughts are normal and

16

everyone has had them at one time or another. I remember I had them after Dad died.

I keep asking myself why and how. Why did this happen? Although you were eighty-three, I never thought you were going to die. You just didn't seem to be sick. I also ask how the doctors could not have known something was wrong. I'm sure your arteries were clogged way before you had the heart attack. How come they never diagnosed it? I keep hoping history could be changed, and you could be saved, but it's too late. You have already passed on. The doctors cannot help you anymore. I still can't believe it. I felt this way all weekend busting up your house. It felt like I was invading your house and going through things which did not belong to me. I guess with each conversation I have I say the same things. I just don't know what to say anymore. I love you, Ma, and will speak to you later. Mel.

Wednesday, September 4, 1996

Hi Ma,

I wish I could say to you, "How are you today?" I think you were robbed of a few years, Ma. You just didn't seem that sick to me. I just can't believe it every time I think about it. I can't believe it! Still, when I used to talk to you about next year, you would say to me, "Let's live until next year!" knowing that you might not. You were all prepared: you had the will done; you put all the papers away so that we could find them; you listed everything for us; you made it easy for us, Ma. You thought of us all the time and were a wonderful person. I asked Bert what was worse for him, when Dad died or now, when you passed away. He said now, because he knew you longer. I guess I could say

17

that's true for me, also. It's hard for me to compare because I was only twelve years old then, and devastated over Dad's death. At least now I can deal with it on an adult level. It still hurts, though. I speak to Alan and Bert on a daily basis and they seem to be doing fine. I just don't think they were as close to you as I was. Maybe that's not the right thing to say, but I was with you more than they were, especially over the last ten years, and we became the best of friends. That's not to say you didn't care for them and love them, and they didn't care for and love you, but we had a special relationship.

I sent a copy of your photo to your brother, Ben. I think he's going to love it. Well, Ma, I have to take a break from this. I will speak to you later. Mel.

Thursday, September 5, 1996 9:05 A.M.

Hi Ma,

I was thinking this morning about dealing with the undertaker after you died. I spoke to him about an hour after you passed away. He asked me if I wanted a shomer to stay with you and say the necessary prayers and, of course, he informed me of how much it would cost. The thing that goes through my mind is the day of the funeral, when I had to settle the bill. No, actually, it was the Friday before. I met Alan and Bert at the chapel to see the funeral director. We got the breakdown of the cost of the funeral. The thing that sticks out in my mind was "refrigeration." They told us how much it cost for "refrigeration." It seemed so callous and cold, just like the word. It was terrible to hear that. I'll talk to you later. Mel.

Thursday, September 5, 1996 11:00 A.M.

Hi Ma,

To know you had to be refrigerated like a piece of meat, that made me feel terrible. I know you couldn't feel anything, but the thought of it was upsetting. Also, we have to pay for that and it was something like $345. It just seemed inappropriate. For the undertakers, of course, it was just routine. I have to go now, so I will talk to you later.

Same day, 2:00 P.M.

It's a little slow at work today, but I'm waiting for a large order from one of my accounts. They are supposed to call this afternoon. I was thinking about Bert and Alan. Bert always went through a "song-and-dance routine" whenever you asked him to do something. I could never understand why he felt these antics were necessary, as he always did it anyway.

As for Alan, it was physically impossible for him to routinely do things for you because he lived so far away. I'm sure if he were closer he would have made an effort to do more.

Sometimes I was also reluctant to do things for you, but I always did them, especially taking you to the supermarket. I know you enjoyed going and it got you out of the house a little while, but Ma, you were a pain in the ass. You had to examine every piece of fruit! You had to compare the prices of every can on the shelves. You drove me crazy! It's no wonder I didn't want to go, but I did. It's funny, you were always afraid of what Kay was going to say, and she used to remind me when it was time to meet

19

you. She used to love having you with us wherever we went.

I know you didn't like me seeing my psychologist, Othello. You used to always say to me, "he didn't cure you yet?" But Ma, talking to him makes me feel better and understand myself better.

I didn't always want to go to your house to eat on Friday nights. After working a whole week I sometimes wanted to go home and do nothing. But even if I told you not to make dinner, you would anyway. Sometimes, I was angry when I went up to your house, and I'm sorry for that behavior. Tomorrow, I will talk to you about the apartment itself and the dreams that I have. Love, Mel.

Thursday, September 5, 1996 4:45 P.M.

Hi Ma,
You know, Ma, when I would say to you, "I don't believe it," you would say to me, "Believe it, believe it." I can hear you saying that to me now, about your death, "Believe it, believe it."

Friday, September 6, 1996 10:30 A.M.

Hi Ma,
I've had three dreams about you already. In the first one, you were falling and I was holding you in my arms. I put you down; I think it was on the floor (I think it has to do when I saw you walk out of the bedroom when we took you to the hospital). You were lying on your left side. I was on my knees facing your back and you turned your

20

head and looked at me and jerked your head and moved your eyes at the same time as if to say, go on and go do what you have to do. It's as if you were saying, go and live your life . . . don't worry about me.

In the second dream, I saw you somewhere; your legs were swollen, but you were alive. The third one was last night. Alan and I went over to your hospital bed. It was a dormitory and when we went over you were getting ready to sit up. Alan said to me, "Look at this!" I thought you were getting better and you were, in the dream, but then I awoke and reality set in.

Monday, September 9, 1996

Hi Ma,
I had another dream. You were in the apartment after we cleared it out. It was Bert and I. I'll talk to you tomorrow about it.

Tuesday, September 10, 1996 5:40 P.M.

Hi Ma,
I'm thinking now about that last dream, and I really can't remember it.

Anyway, we cleared your house out over the weekend. The house is almost completely empty now. I never thought I would see it like this. It was difficult for me, but I did it. Alan said he couldn't do it. Bert helped as much as he was able to. Most of your furniture was taken by Kay's family. As I told you, Kay's nephew is getting married and wanted a lot of things. They are starting fresh

21

and it will help them. Kay's sister, Johanna, took Baba's breakfront, the crystal lamp that you loved, and a few other lamps and pictures. You know Johanna, she loves these kinds of antique furnishings, so they couldn't be in better hands. My friend Alice Meyer asked if I had a large pot to give her for when she makes stuffed cabbage for the holidays, so I gave her the largest pot you had. She was really thrilled with it. Many of your other household belongings went to family members who would appreciate them and now have something to remember you by. There are a lot of other items I just didn't have the heart to give away. They are things that bring back memories of you, memories that I want to hold on to. I don't want to let go of you, but I know I have to. There are still a lot of your papers and things I have to go through and make a decision about. Right now, all of this stuff is in my apartment and it looks like a bomb hit it.

I remember when I spoke to Dr. Schwartz in the hospital and he told me that you almost died on Tuesday, July 23, the night he had you moved to another hospital. I don't know if you had another heart attack that night. I'm still groping for answers, but I just don't seem to get the ones that I want.

Tomorrow, I want to talk to you about the cemetery and when we buried you. Well, I have to go now, Ma. I love you and will speak to you later. Love, Mel.

Wednesday, September 11, 1996

Hi Ma,
The dirt hitting the box. That was horrible to listen to. I was the first one to throw dirt onto your coffin. The

sound was ominous. I asked the rabbi if women could throw dirt; he said yes, and Kay was the first of the women to do it. I ended up crying on the shoulder of the dentist's wife, Marlene, who is Alan's friend. She was very nice and tried to console me. It was tough that day. I never really thought of what that day would be like: watching them put the coffin in the grave; throwing the dirt onto the coffin; the dirt hitting the coffin; the workers wanting to use the backhoe to finish covering the coffin; feeling horrified at the coldness of using a backhoe; the rabbi saying no to the backhoe; thanking him; waiting for the whole casket to be covered by dirt; the rabbi performing the prayer service; saying Kaddish; walking through the crowd back to the cars; going back to your house; serving appetizers; and starting the one-week period of sitting shivah.

There were a lot of people in the house the first couple of days. Toward the end of the week it slowed down, but people came all week long. There were a lot of people at the cemetery and chapel for the eulogy and most of these people came back to the house.

It was a difficult day for Alan, Bert and me; for Sharon, Gail and Kay and your grandchildren, and everybody else that loved you. I guess I never thought the day would come when we would be going to the cemetery to take you there for other than visiting Dad and your parents. Now I have to go visit all of you. It's going to be tough.

Anyway, on another note, our contractor came up to the house and had some ideas about fixing it up. I'll have to talk to you about this later. It's getting late and I want to go home. Also, I have to have a conversation with Dad. It's time after thirty-two years. I love you, Mel.

Thursday, September 12, 1996

Well, hello, Dad,

I never communicated with you in this fashion. I can't say that I've never spoken to you, but I never wrote down a conversation on paper as I've been doing with Mama this last month. I guess you know by now that Mama has died. She had a heart attack and went through open-heart surgery, which she survived. It was after the operation when she ran into trouble. I wonder how it felt for you to be with her again. I wonder if you were able to sit down and have a conversation and get to know each other again. All I could hope for is that if you two did meet again, it was a happy time for both of you.

Dad, my life changed dramatically after you died. I hated it, I was angry and I was depressed. Because you were not around to teach me, I grew to hate myself. I became overweight, which was a symptom of the way I felt. Nobody could replace you. You were my life and at a critical time you were taken away. Mama tried her best to make me feel better; she provided for, cared for, nurtured and nourished me. But these things couldn't take the place of what I needed when I was twelve years old. I needed someone I could identify with, and you were that person. I guess I could say, after you died, I lost my identity.

Something you left me, which I love, is my feeling for art, whether it be music (by the way, I study classical guitar and am thinking of studying the instrument you played, the violin), paintings, or movies, etc. You taught me how to see the beauty in it, to look at a beautiful sunset and appreciate it. This is what you gave to me. Dad, you were a beautiful man. You always took me to museums, just you and I. It was our time together. You also took me to baseball games. We saw Sandy Koufax, of the Dodgers, pitch against the New York Mets. And I'll never forget our annual visits to Macy's Thanksgiving Day Parade. You used to always find a spot on 34th Street, right on a manhole cover, so we'd stay warm from the steam. Then you would leave me there and go buy a hot chocolate for me and a coffee for you. I loved those days. You were my connection to the outside world.

According to Alan and Bert, you had a bad temper and would hit them. I wonder if that anger came from your sisters because I think they hurt you and Mom. By the time I was growing up, you had calmed down. I remember your hitting me just one time. I failed a test and you gave me one quick hit in the arm with a book. After you died, I spent the next thirteen years searching for a father figure, which I didn't find until I went for professional help and found Othello. I've been seeing him for a long time and just realized that maybe I've been seeing him so long because if you were alive, wouldn't I have been seeing you? Please explain that to Mama. Maybe she'll understand now why I see O. She didn't understand when I told her. She thought it was a waste of money. He helped me understand things that you would have taught me if you had lived. Now that I am a grown man, have I ever gotten over your death? I would say that I have. Of course, that scar on my heart is always there, but the passing years have allowed healing scar tissue to form and cover it. Mama's scar is a different story; it's still fresh and raw. I can't believe how easy it is to tell you all of these things. I hope you are hearing them. I will talk to you again. I love you, and have always missed you. Love, Mel.

Friday, September 13, 1996 11:00 A.M.

Hi Ma,

It's Mel. It's the eve of Rosh Hashanah and you would be preparing meals for the holidays, or making "Yontif," as you would call it. Tomorrow, we're going to Alan's. He will have the holiday meal in his house and Bert, Gail, Lisa and Gail's father will be there. I feel sad today because the holidays, a time of reflection on the past, are making me feel that way. But the holidays are also a time when everyone looks ahead to the future, hoping that his or her name will be written in the book of life and he or she will live another year. But as you know, like when you pointed up to the sky from the hospital bed, it's in God's hands. He decides. I will go to Shul tonight and basically all weekend to pray and say Kaddish. This is the first time I will be celebrating the holidays without you, and it won't be the same. Your death has changed things. We have to ask for atonement for our sins for this entire holiday period. It starts with Rosh Hashanah and culminates with Yom Kippur. It is a ten-day period of penitence and prayer, for looking at oneself, looking at the world, thinking about the future, and generally just being solemn. It's a serious holiday with life and death implications. I remember you used to say who knows what next year will bring, let's live until next year. Well, you didn't live until next year. I think you were robbed of a few years, but as I said before, who am I to ask questions? I will miss you this holiday. I wish you were here to celebrate it with us. Love, Mel.

Monday, September 16, 1996 2:30 P.M.

Hi Ma,

It's Mel.   Everything went okay in Alan's house Saturday night.   Everybody was there, and talking, and friendly; you would've been happy. I hope you saw from wherever you are. It wasn't the same for me without you; there was a void at the dinner table. It seemed like a happy time with an air of sadness in it. Alan started telling stories about you and started to cry.

A friend of mine named Paul told me I didn't seem happy the last few times he saw me. I told him that was true, that after you lose a parent, an aura of sadness envelopes you and changes you emotionally. I guess it's just a symptom of still being in shock. It will take a while for me to get back to being normal. He told me he doesn't know how it feels . . . he never lost a parent. I guess I can speak from experience, because now I have lost you and Dad. Alan said the difference between your and Dad's passing was that Dad was so young. He had a heart attack in the middle of the night and died thirty-two years ago. I guess we were with you for a much longer time and that makes a difference. Anyway, I went to Shul all weekend and said Kaddish. I have been using my tallis, the one your Aunt Esther bought me for my Bar Mitzvah. You know, Ma, I remember you came home from work, it was winter, and we got the notice from the post office that it had come and I wanted it, so you went back out to the post office and got it for me. That made me happy. I keep thinking of the things you did for me through my life, and it was always with love. You always wanted your children to be happy and you always took care of us.

27

Today I saw that new doctor that I mentioned before, Dr. Stein, for treatment of the mild flare-up of MS I have had since your death. He told me not to worry about it at this point, but just to keep an eye on it. He wants me to go for another MRI just to see what's going on. Well, I'll talk to you later. Love, Mel.

Monday, September 16, 1996, 4:45 P.M.

Hi Ma,

Alan keeps telling me that after he saw you in the hospital he knew you wouldn't come out. He told me he told this to Bert. This is upsetting to me. I don't know why he said that. Actually, I do know why, and maybe he's not wrong. He said you looked so skinny; you had lost so much weight. I guess maybe he was preparing himself for the worst. I know that he loved you. Because I saw you every day, I guess I just didn't notice that you were as sick as you were.

There were times when he called you and you wouldn't answer the phone. He would call me and ask me where you were, and on occasion say, "I thought this was it." I guess it was probably always on his mind that this would happen to you. I'll talk to you later, Mel.

Tuesday, September 17, 1996, 4:45 P.M.

Hi Ma,

It's Mel. It has been an irritating day. The nonsense things seem to be the most irritating, but as you used to say, "That's what it is."

There's not a day that goes by that I don't think about you, what you went through, and why it had to be so tough on you. And yet, Dr. Stein told me yesterday you had it good. He has seen patients linger on and suffer. I know you would not have wanted that.

I remember there were times when I would sit in your living room and think that someday your apartment would

29

be mine. People don't live forever and I knew this time would come. I just did not think it would be now. As I keep saying, I just wasn't ready for it to happen. I thought and really believed you would live until age ninety. I just didn't think you were sick. But now that it has happened, Ma, I'm glad I don't feel guilty about getting your apartment, because I know you wanted me to have it. But Ma, I can't help wondering what you'll think when you see what we're going to do to it. It's really going to be beautiful, and I think you'll like it.

You know, Ma, the only problem with these conversations is, you can't answer me back. I looked up the word *conversation* in the dictionary and it said, "an informal spoken exchange." That explains it. There is no conversation. These are more like letters to you. I like to write them because they make me feel better. These letters are my catharsis. Well, I'm going to go home in a couple of minutes so I will talk to you later. Love, Mel.

Wednesday, September 18, 1996

Dear Ma,
My new format will be letters, not conversations.

As executor of your estate, I have been settling all your financial affairs. I can imagine the complexities of settling a large estate, considering the work involved in settling yours, and I still have to finish the estate tax returns.

Going through your papers is a very personal thing for me. Those things that I have found that have meaning for me I am keeping. I found your wedding invitation, and the menu of the food served at your wedding. I couldn't help but wonder what you and Dad had for dinner that night and whether you both enjoyed your wedding celebration. I found Dad's citizenship papers and his social security card. All these things I am keeping. Many papers I am throwing out because I really have no need for them, such as old bank statements and tax information from years ago. I remember you kept asking me if you could throw away all the old papers. There were also photos of Alan, Bert and me as well as lots of family photos. We'll split these among the three of us.

You know, Ma, I'm just thinking that maybe I changed to Dear Ma, from Hi Ma, it's Mel, because I'm starting to accept your death. But as I write it, a funny feeling comes over me, that feeling of disbelief, as how could it be possible that you died when you were so very much alive and alert? Anyway, I'm going through many papers. It's a pretty daunting task. It's a process I have to go through, and as I do it, I chip away at your life. It seems that everything I do is a process. So life is all these processes that we've gone through over the years, which adds up to connected processes, which is life. So you've been through all these processes in your life from the time you were born, grew up, went to school, married Dad, had children, went through Dad's death, went to work, supported and took care of your family, had knee surgery, had open-heart surgery, died, and of course, everything in between. All these were processes over time. Are time and processes the same thing? "A series of steps, actions or operations used to bring about a desired result, a series of natural changes by which something passes from one condition to another," is what the dictionary says about *process*. *Time*, in the dictionary, is described as follows: "A nonspatial continuum in which events occur in apparently irreversible succession. An interval separating two points on this continuum; duration." If they don't mean the same thing, they are certainly interrelated. I can hear you saying, "I don't understand." You know, Ma, I'm not sure I understand it myself! Well anyway, I'll write to you again tomorrow. I love you, Mel.

Thursday, September 19, 1996

Dear Ma,
I'm tired today. I've been up late going through your papers. I am throwing out most of them.

Business is good this week. I may get a large order from one of my customers, which would double my sales. It seems as time goes on, I am getting used to the fact that you are not here anymore. Sometimes I forget about it and when I realize that, I feel guilty. I'm sure that's normal. The mind wants to move on to other things. I can't stay sad and depressed all of the time. One just naturally starts to come out of it after a while. That's not to say that I forgot what happened to you, just that I started to think about other things, and getting busy at work helps. When I have time to reflect, that's when I realize what I'm missing. It makes me sad to know I can't talk to you anymore. I liked talking to you. You understood so much about life. Anyway, I will be going home soon, so I will speak to you tomorrow.

Friday, September 20, 1996

Dear Ma,
Yom Kippur falls out on a Monday this year and Bob is going to close the office, which is good because I wouldn't

have gone to work anyway. I will be in Shul all day, praying and trying to fast, although I seem to have a problem completing it. We'll see what happens.

Josie is dizzy all the time. It has made her very depressed. Actually, I think it's adding to a depression that's already there. She can't seem to keep herself occupied with things. She's having trouble accepting her fate, and she seems bored and lethargic. This is a woman that has dedicated herself to taking care of her family, but the family is not around on a daily basis anymore. Except for Kay and me, she doesn't see her kids that often. She cooks dinner for us almost every night. When I don't go up there, Kay does, and of course I would never stop her from seeing her parents. You used to say to me you can't. You're right, Ma, I can't and I wouldn't. Josie seems to need a hobby. Sitting in the house all day is making her depressed. I'm sure the dizziness is very uncomfortable for her. What I don't understand is, when Kay and I want to take her to eat or to do something, she doesn't want to go. A perfect example is the Bermuda cruise. Ma, you would've loved to go, and you said so. Not Josie. She just isn't that excited about it. Maybe she doesn't want to let go of the past, but one can't live in the past. One has to look forward to the future, no matter what age. Josie doesn't even want to go see another doctor about the dizziness. She doesn't think it will help. Ma, you used to say that she needed more outside activities. You often asked Josie to join you when you visited the ladies' club, but she never did. She just can't seem to find something that will occupy her time although she says she would like to. How could she be motivated? That is the question. Well anyway, I have to go. I'll write you again later or tomorrow.

Tuesday, September 24, 1996

Dear Ma,

I missed seeing you this weekend. It was Yom Kippur and I would've been up to your house on this holiday. I went to Shul just about all weekend long. It was a long, drawn-out affair, but I'm glad I did it. I said Kaddish for you and Yizkor for Dad. I always look in the Shul where Dad's name is on the plaque. Saul Mark made a space for you and said he would make up a plaque for you after the holidays, just as you wanted. I made donations in the Shul throughout the holiday, and gave a generous amount. You would probably say, "you're crazy!," but the Shul needs the money. Anyway, I'm glad I did.

I talked to Alan over the weekend and we both felt that it didn't seem that you were ready to die. I told him, as I said before, that I thought you would live to ninety years old.

Well, anyway, I have to meet Ethel Mark tonight. She is going to take many of your pots and pans for her flea market. Ma, I have to go. I'll write to you tomorrow.

Wednesday, September 25, 1996 11:00 A.M.

Dear Ma,

Bert just called me and told me Aunt Lilly died. She was smoking in bed and the bed caught on fire. She was badly burned. She passed away last night or this morning. I just wanted to tell you this. I'll speak to you later.

Wednesday, September 25, 1996 2:30 P.M.

Dear Ma,

I was just thinking how you used to go up to Aunt Lilly's and Aunt Rose's house to help them. After all that Dad's sisters put you through, and all they had done to you, you went up to their house to help them. Ma, you were a saint.

Thursday, September 26, 1996

Dear Ma,

I spoke to Bert a little while ago and he told me only he and cousin Charlene were at Aunt Lilly's funeral (I can only hope that she and Dad are now at peace with each other). I just thought about the difference when compared to your funeral. At your funeral there must've been 200 people; the whole neighborhood paid respects. I know that Aunt Lilly gave you a hard time in your life, but I could hear you say that you would never wish her any harm. You used to tell me that Baba would always say, "You can't wish harm on a person because you may be wishing it on yourself." Now all that's left of Dad's family are Aunt Rose and Charlene.

I don't know if I told you I spoke to your brother, Ben, yesterday. He said everything was fine. He has a problem with his back, but I think he's going to take steroids for it. I told him that Dad's sister, Lilly, died, but he really didn't have much to say, except that he was sorry.

At work today, Bob was telling me that he believes people become reunited. He doesn't know on what plane that occurs, but he believes it. He said that your senses don't give you a true picture of reality, and that to really understand and to see the way things are you have to go beyond your senses. But people don't believe certain things because they don't realize it through their senses, so that, if you don't sense it, you don't believe it. I also believe that, sometime, somewhere and somehow, I will be reunited with you, because I believe I can go beyond, and have gone beyond, my senses. I hope so, because I would give anything to talk to you again. How's Dad doing? I hope he's doing fine after all these years. I guess if you are in Paradise, you are in a much better place than here. I miss talking with you. I know I keep saying that, but it's true. We're making arrangements to have the apartment redone. Tonight, after work, I'm going to meet Kay to look at kitchen cabinets. Ma, I'll talk to you again tomorrow. Love, Mel.

Friday, September 27, 1996

Dear Ma,

It's Friday, the weekend is here, and we don't have much planned. We have to make one last trip to Goodwill to take some of your things. Ethel Mark came up to my house and took the pots and pans, all your knitting instructions, some dishes, etc. She said she will be able to sell them in the flea market. I think that's the same flea market you took Stacey to once. We have to go look at some tile this weekend. The kitchen cabinets we saw last night gave us an idea of what we want. It's going to take time to have the apartment constructed the way we want it.

I spoke to cousin Dennis before. He told me he was doing okay. He's collecting SSI and is trying to get disability from the insurance company. I hope it works out for him. He says Aunt Natalie is doing fine. She has to have surgery to remove her cataracts.

Time seems to be moving very rapidly. From the time we left on vacation for Alaska until now, I don't know where it has gone. It's been almost three months since I went to Alaska, and everything since then seems like a blur.

We have to try to straighten out our apartment this weekend, because it's still full of your stuff. I'm still going through your papers and will have more to throw out. Anyway, life is going on because time doesn't stop for anybody.

Business was good this week and I just hope it keeps up. Tonight you would be going down to play Mah Jongg in the club, but it seems that the ladies don't play so much anymore. They told me they miss you, and so far, they haven't found a suitable replacement. I know what they're talking about. Mel.

Monday, September 30, 1996

Dear Ma,
Tomorrow it will be two months since you died. Those thoughts of you in the hospital keep creeping into my head. Seeing you after the operation, writing notes to each other before the operation, those thoughts are still distressing. How does one explain death? Does it ever become an understandable event? Everybody knows about it. Everybody knows that they are going to die at some time, but people want to hold onto life for as long as they can. You wrote on the pad to me in the hospital, "Will I be able

to speak again?" (you were making reference to the tube down your throat). You were thinking about after you got out of the hospital. I know I've said somewhere before that you knew what the score was, but did you really consider the outcome? I don't think people do that. I think people go on living and think they will keep living, until they cannot think anymore. I think this occurs no matter what a person's condition is. I don't think that you thought you would die. You probably considered that it might happen, but did you really, really believe it? I think it happens when it happens and a person just doesn't know about it.

Let me get back to reality. Your house is completely cleared out and the contractor is ready to come in and start breaking down walls. I will talk to him tonight and get a price for the work, including the demolition. He met with the cabinetmaker today to computerize a plan for the kitchen. We started looking at tile for the kitchen floor and for the bathroom.

My car was damaged in the parking lot. The parking lot sidewalk is being fixed and the repairmen hit the side of my car with their truck. I spoke to a representative in the management office today, and was told to call back next week.

A day does not go by when I do not think about you. Anyway, I have to go now, but I will write to you again tomorrow. Love, Mel.

Tuesday, October 1, 1996

Dear Ma,

It's Tuesday, October 1, 1996. I have my first guitar lesson tonight. I usually feel excited about that, but this year I'm not. The sadness of your not being here is always with me. It surrounds me all the time, no matter what I do. I thought the passage of time would change that feeling, but it hasn't. Maybe it's too soon and more time has to pass. The contractor is coming over to the house tonight (your house) and we are going to try to finalize the work we want to do.

I had a busy day at the office today. It's funny how on busy days, such as today, I am able to work although I'm still in mourning. I remember that I worked in the mornings of the week we sat shivah, and even then I was able to take the sales orders. Somehow one must rise to the occasion and just do what's necessary.

Saturday, I got called up to the Torah to make an aliyah. It felt good. You always used to ask me if I could read Hebrew, well, I can; not perfectly, but not bad. There is something I wanted to talk to you about . . . and it's bothering me because I can't remember what it is. I don't think we discussed it before. Anyway, I have to go to my lesson. I'll write again. Love, Mel.

Wednesday, October 2, 1996

Dear Ma,

There have been some changes in Kay's life today. Kay's immediate boss (by the way, she was at your funeral) has given her notice at work. In the meantime, the contractor just called to tell me they broke down the walls in your house. Getting back to what I was talking about, Kay is depressed about her boss's leaving and has a decision to make. She was offered a management position but isn't sure she wants it or even to stay at this job. She doesn't really like the work she is doing and the atmosphere at this place, according to Kay, is depressing.

All I know is, Kay deserves a break. She should be able to do something that she likes to do. If she accepts this job, I don't think she will like it and she doesn't want the extra responsibility. I don't think it's worth the money (she would get an increase). The morale of the employees is really low, which affects work productivity and relationships between employees, and creates an extremely poor working environment. I know, Ma, I could hear you saying, "It's not for me to understand. Do what you think is best." Anyway, I'll talk to you tomorrow. Love, Mel.

Thursday, October 3, 1996

Dear Ma,
You should see your apartment. The living room wall, the wall between the kitchen and the dining room, and Baba's closet are gone. The apartment has a whole different look to it. You wouldn't recognize it if you saw it.

I was thinking today how I never considered you to be old. I knew it and understood it, but never considered it. I guess when one is with a person for so many years he starts to take certain things for granted, such as, his parents are always going to be there. One thinks his parents are always the same, that they never change. He knows intellectually that they change, but not emotionally. I guess what I'm trying to say is for me, you were stuck in time. You always stayed the same, no matter how many years passed by. You never got old; you never got young; you were always the same. I really didn't realize that you changed until you died. Maybe that's it. You changed because you're physically not here anymore. Because if you were alive, as I said before, you would not have changed.

Business is still pretty good. I hope it keeps up. Alan is retiring soon, and Bert called me. He wants to buy a new car. I spoke to both of them today. Love, Mel.

Friday, October 4, 1996

Dear Ma,

Alan and Bert did a very nice thing for me. They said if I needed to borrow their share of your inheritance to fix up the apartment that I could do it, and I may have to. I'm having trouble working out the financing on my own, therefore, I may take them up on their offer.

Ma, you just wouldn't believe the way your apartment looks, it's that different. The whole area is opened up and it's going to look beautiful. I hope so, anyway. It's costing a bundle, but I would rather do it now, while the apartment is empty. We want to move in with the apartment completely done.

I'm tired today because I didn't get a good night's sleep. Tonight I have to go to the synagogue for Friday evening services. I saw Saul Mark this morning while I was going to work, and it reminded me to talk to him about

41

placing your remembrance plaque in the synagogue next to Dad's. They should start doing that soon.

I still have many of your papers to go through and it looks like most of them will be thrown out.

I still don't see how it's possible that you died! When I look at your photo on top of the piano, it looks as if your lips are moving and you are talking. You had such a nice white color to your hair. I liked your hair. When you were sick in the hospital and I was petting your head, strands of your hair would fall out into my hand. Kay had told me in the hospital to cut off a lock of your hair, but for some reason I didn't want to do that. Ma, I miss you very much. I know I'll never get a chance to talk to you again. Death is such a final thing, but that is what it is.

It's the weekend and we won't be doing too much. Kay said she wanted to stay home and relax. She had a rough week with the changes in her office. Ma, I'm going to go now. I'll speak to you on Monday. Love, Mel.

October 7, 1996

Dear Ma,

You would've been proud of me this weekend. It was Simchas Torah and I was in Shul both Saturday and Sunday. I made an aliyah and carried the Torah. Although the services are sometimes a little long, I like going. The men in the synagogue read much faster than I do and it's difficult to keep up. One man in the synagogue, Joe, is very helpful. When I first started going to the synagogue he would show me how to find the prayers in the book, and he kept an eye on me to make sure I didn't lose my place.

He told me that you were looking down on me and was proud and happy at what you saw. I hope it's true, Ma, because I always wanted to make you proud of me. I also helped Saul by taking donation pledges and calling out the names and the amounts. After everybody left, I helped Saul clean up. The people want a synagogue but it's sad that nobody offers any assistance. Thank God for Saul and Ethel because without them there would be no synagogue. At least, that's how it appears to me.

The weekend was otherwise very quiet. We stayed home and didn't do much. We went up to the apartment and took some photos of the walls torn down and we discussed how we would like the kitchen to look.

Bert wanted to buy a new car, but felt that it was too soon after your death to get one. He asked me what I thought and I told him that you would have said, "If it's good for you, it's good for me, but if you think I'm giving you any money, you've got a good case!" I told him, in other words, not to feel guilty and to get it, so he did. I have to go now (it's time to get to work). I'll write to you later. Love, Mel.

October 8, 1996

Dear Ma,

The cooperators are voting this week on whether or not to reconstitute our housing development. By Friday we should know the results. It's really a better deal for everybody if it passes. Reconstitution, while raising the value of each apartment, would put a cap on the value in order to allow the apartments to remain accessible to middle-class families, which constitute the majority of the development. There is a faction of people who are opposed to reconstitution because they feel there should not be a cap placed on the value of the apartments. However, the board of directors made it clear that the cap would be reviewed in the future. I feel that the faction of people who are trying to defeat the decision don't understand what's being done and they're being greedy about it. Well, I hope it passes. I'll let you know what happens.

I've been thinking today, again, how I would like to talk to you. I've been fantasizing about going to a seance and seeing if I can get in contact with you. I just wish that I could talk to you again.

It's raining in the city today and they expect it to come down even harder. It reminds me of when I was in Alaska and one Saturday when I called you, you said " . . . the rain is coming down unbelievable!"

As of tomorrow, Alan will be a retiree, because today is his last day at work. I remember you used to tell me that Alan always spoke to you about it, and you said, "When it will happen, it will happen." I wish you were alive to see this momentous occasion in Alan's life. I hope Alan enjoys it because he's been talking about it forever.

Ma, it's pouring outside so I think I'm going to leave. Maybe I'll be able to catch a cab. Love, Mel.

October 9, 1996

Dear Ma,

I'm being very careful not to say I have to call you because I'm trying to get myself to realize that you are not

44

here anymore. I was thinking about your heart today; about how badly damaged it must have looked after the heart attack. I never knew that the heart has an empty space in it, but I just read somewhere that it does. Anyway, after thinking all these thoughts, I always wind up wondering why your heart was so badly damaged. Why couldn't it be that your heart was NOT badly damaged and you had a chance to live?

The contractor was up to the house yesterday and removed the bathtub. Kay and I met Dora and we brought her up to the house to see it. She couldn't believe what she saw. As I told you before, it looks like a different apartment. Ma, I can't write any more because I'm very tired. I'll talk to you tomorrow. Love, Mel.

October 10, 1996

Dear Ma,

I found myself shaking my head today thinking about you. It reminded me of when you were in the hospital. I saw you looking up and shaking your head. It seemed you were saying, *what the hell happened to me?* You didn't see me looking at you. That thought hurts me.

You know, Ma, I just realized how deeply I love you. I cared for you so much that I felt that I had to protect you and didn't want anything to happen to you. I always had a fear that something would. I had a fear that when you were in the street you might get mugged and hurt, and I couldn't stand to see you hurt. Those thoughts made me nervous then. But, you know, I still have them. What does that mean? Am I living in an alternate universe? Am I living in a dream thinking you're alive when you're not? It seems that I fantasize about the way I want it to be, but I can't have my way; you're gone.

People have told me that after their parents died, they felt as if a load was taken off their shoulders and they didn't have a burden anymore. Who knows? Maybe their parents were burdens. As for me, you were never a burden. As a matter of fact, Kay and I miss having you with us. I miss telling you that you were a pain in the neck, and having you tell me, "So are you!" It was fun being with you. I tried to be good to you and think that I was on many occasions. Kay and I always took you with us, and I think you enjoyed being with us. I hope you did. I know, when we always took you home, you were happy to get there. You used to say, "Home sweet home, be it ever so humble."

I think about Dad and wonder about the kind of relationship I would've had with him over the last thirty years. You and I always had a good relationship. We had some rough spots, but that was generational. You were always there for me whenever I needed you. I'll write to you later. Love, Mel.

October 11-12, 1996

Dear Ma,

I wish I could ask you how you feel, the way I used to. Kay just said you would say, "Kvetching along." You know, Ma, I remember when the doctor asked you to sign the paper giving permission to operate. You were so disgusted with your illness that you just signed to get it over with. You signed the paper and made a waving gesture of dismissal with your hand. The doctor wanted to tell you about everything that you were signing, but you didn't want to hear it. You know, Ma, it felt to me that you were signing away your life. I guess that's what happened.

You'd be happy to know that reconstitution passed by 81% in favor. I'm glad because now remodeling the apartment will make it that much more valuable.

We were out to Alan's Saturday night for a dinner party with friends and family. It was an enjoyable evening. I hope Alan realizes that since he just retired it's a novelty being home and eventually he's got to do something. I was thinking about how Alan supported us after Dad died. I know he gave you his entire pay until you got on your feet. He gave me money every week and told me, "I don't want you to be without any money." He also gave me money when I went to Europe the last couple of years I was in college. I don't forget things like that. He cared about us and I can't help but love him for it. He told me that he was proud of me for taking care of you; well, I'm proud of him for taking care of us. You told me, Ma, when Dad died you were earning $45 per week at the Metropolitan Life Insurance Company and Alan really supported us. I didn't realize this until I was old enough to understand, and all I could say is, without him, I don't know what would've happened.

The apartment is coming along beautifully. I wish you could see it. Love, Mel.

October 15, 1996

Dear Ma,

I spoke to your brother, Ben, today. He said that his back was bothering him and the doctors are giving him cortisone injections to alleviate the pain. You know, it's funny; years ago I was angry at him. He gave you all kinds of advice about me, without ever understanding where I was at. He never once asked me about what I was feeling. But, now that I'm older, I realize what I was really angry about was that Dad wasn't there to guide me, and I shouldn't have expected your brother to replace him. It wasn't really my uncle's fault. He cared, but he had his own family to take care of. It's nice to talk to him now, and I sense that he is happy and appreciates it when I call him.

We were in the house last night, and as I was looking around, it dawned on me that there was a comparison to be made between you and the apartment. There were telltale signs that you were coming to the end. Your body started breaking down and with it, the apartment. You really couldn't take care of it anymore. It was beyond you, a physical impossibility. I remember I used to get upset and angry with you when I came in the house, and saw it deteriorating, and that was wrong. This ties in with what I said a few days ago; that I never realized you had changed. You always stayed the same to me, so I expected everything to stay the same. I guess it was stupid for me to think like that, but the subtle changes sneaked up on me when I was not looking. Only recently I realized the metamorphosis that had occurred. Anyway, I have to go to a guitar lesson so I will talk to you tomorrow. Love, Mel.

October 16, 1996

Dear Ma,

I was thinking about the last time I saw you. They had reduced your oxygen intake and it looked like you were having trouble breathing. I wish I had not seen you like that. You were dying. That look was on your face. You died about six hours after that. There was just nothing they could do to help you. They tried everything. The medicines weren't working. Your body was just giving out. When I look at your photo on the piano, it makes me sad to know I can't see you anymore. By the way, on the days I don't go to the synagogue, I say Kaddish in front of this photo of you.

Kay and I are going through your photos, and there are some wonderful ones of you and Dad when you were both young, before Alan was born. There are also photos of us when we were children, some of Bert and Alan when you lived in the Bronx, and some of people I don't even know. But I can't find the photo of my grandfather Charles, you know, the one you showed me of him standing on a stoop. But I'll keep looking.

I'm almost finished going through your papers; I'm up to the recipes. I hope we can duplicate some of the meals you made as I used to enjoy them very much.

Alan says so far he's enjoying his retirement. At this point, it's like a vacation for him, and I hope he has no problem adjusting in the future.

I don't have anything else to say today, except I think I'm coming down with something. I have a headache and don't feel well. I'll talk to you tomorrow. Love, Mel.

October 17, 1996

Dear Ma,

I was just thinking about the Friday night before we came home from Alaska. I called you and you answered the phone with some vigor. It sounded like you were feeling great and maybe you were at that moment. It's too bad it didn't last for long because, by the end of the weekend, you were really sick. Bert said when he came up to see you Saturday night, you seemed to be doing fine, so you must have gotten sick after that. These thoughts have crossed my mind this morning and I know I've spoken to you about them before. I'm still hoping things could've worked out differently. It doesn't hurt to dream, does it? I'll talk to you later. Love, Mel.

October 21, 1996

Dear Ma,

Sorry I never got back to you on Friday, but it was very busy in the office. I had a dream about you last night, and it's like every other dream I've had about you: in the end you are always alive and well. In the dream you were cooking and I was standing beside you. All I could think of was that the operation was successful and you didn't die. There was also a baby in the dream, walking near you, but I don't know what that means, if anything. Maybe they're my memories of when I was a baby.

Writing to you reminds me of when I was in Europe. The letters you would write to me were like diary entries of your day. It seems that I do some of that now that I am writing to you.

We were supposed to go to New Jersey on Saturday to celebrate Anthony's first birthday, (Anthony is Kay's grand nephew, Barbara and Patty's grandson), but there was a major rainstorm, so we ended up staying home. It gave me a chance to finish going through all your papers, but there are still more photos to go through. I'm still trying to divide the photos into three equal piles: one for Alan, one for Bert and one for myself. Kay is helping me sort through the photos as it's quite a job.

The construction in the apartment is coming along fine, although the contractor told us it will still be a couple of months before we could move in. We have to choose the tile we want for the kitchen and the bathroom. We have decided to extend the kitchen floor out into the dining area, all the way to the front door. We're even putting it in the hall closet. It should look great. We also have to decide on the kitchen cabinets we want so they can start to build them. It takes about eight weeks to finish making them, so we have to make up our minds right away. We have a good idea of what we want them to be; we know the type of design we want on the cabinet doors and that we want them to be light in color.

You have been on my mind a lot today, and I feel sad. I miss you. Today it seems especially so. I don't know why, but maybe it's the weather. In June when I play at my guitar recital, I'm going to play a piece for you. It's a prayer they sing in the synagogue called, "Avinu Malkaynu." I sang it for my guitar teacher, Silas, and he liked it so much, he's going to write an arrangement of it.

I have to close out your checkbook. Every time I do something such as this, it's like another nail in the coffin, another sign you have died. Maybe that's why I'm sad today. All I know is that you have been on my mind. I'll talk to you later. Love, Mel.

October 22, 1996

Dear Ma,

Bert is doing a lot to help everybody in the family. He directed Kay's résumé to the right people so she can be considered for other positions. He arranged for his boss to meet with Jason. His boss has connections and maybe can get Jason into a hospital in New York when the time comes.

Bert, without knowing it, taught me to be a good salesman. He is the best salesman around. He's so personable that when he talks to people, they like him immediately. It's a terrific quality.

I keep thinking of the doctors sticking that tube down your throat, and it hurts to think of that. The worst thing was that you could not talk to us. The thoughts of you in the hospital are the ones that are lingering and I can't seem to put them out of my mind. Maybe I don't want to because I think they can still save you, so I keep reliving the same sequence of events, only hoping for a different outcome.

Thinking back over the last couple of years, I can now see the way your body started to break down. First it was your hearing, then your knees, then the cataracts in your eyes. Finally, your heart gave out. You had clogged arteries. We never had a clue. These were all signs that your body was breaking down and as a result, you were having trouble living a normal life. Did I not want to see what was going on? I think I saw it, but I didn't recognize it as the beginning of the end. I still think I'm in shock over losing you. Every time I think about you, or look at your photo on the piano, I can't believe that this happened.

I think about death, and wonder if there is life after death. I know some people claim to have had "life after death" experiences. My therapist Othello told me there is a woman who claims she can see people, or communicate with people, after they are dead. I might go to see her. I feel that I have to speak to you again. I know I can't, but I feel I have to. If you knew how troubled I was by your death, and you knew I wanted to talk to you again, if it were possible, I know you would communicate with me. But maybe you can't, or maybe it's too soon; maybe life after death is the memory we have for you. It's a question that might not have an answer.

I'll talk to you tomorrow.

Tell Dad the Yankees won the first game of the World Series. or does he already know this? Does he already know the ultimate outcome? Love, Mel.

October 25, 1996

Dear Ma,

I just thought about the last time I saw you in the hospital, which was the night before you died. It makes me very sad to have seen you like that. It looked like you had patches under your eyes and they were hanging down. I'm extremely upset now thinking about that because I had never seen you in such a terrible state. I feel the pain in my heart even now. I had to watch you and was not able to do anything about it. I'm sorry, Ma, to know that there is nothing I can do about it, that look on your face, the look of death. I don't think you knew what was happening. I feel like crying right now. I don't know why at this moment. It's been almost three months since you died. When I have these thoughts, the pain just comes right back. It's a hard thing to accept. I'll talk to you more, later.

I feel better now. The men are working in the apartment every day. They put halogen lights all over the kitchen and it's coming along beautifully. There will be plenty of light in there, which is exactly what Kay and I wanted.

The artwork we purchased at an auction and had taken to the store to be framed is now ready to be picked up. The needlepoint you made for us, which I had framed previously, was also fixed so that your initials show. I'm glad you made it for us. I feel it's something we have that is part of you. I will put it in a special place in the apartment when we get there.

It's Friday and tonight I will try to make it to the synagogue to say Kaddish, but it will be close. Praying starts at ten minutes after candle lighting, which is 5:44 p.m.

Tomorrow we are supposed to go to south Jersey to see Barbara and Patty. It's nice to see them, but I don't feel like making the trip and that's the reason I don't want to go.

Business is good and I hope it keeps up, especially now, because we will need more money to pay for all this construction being done to your apartment. Also, the rent is going to be higher. I know I've discussed these things with you before, but I think about them, so I talk about them.

Kay is going on many job interviews. I hope she receives a good job offer. She deserves it. I'm going to go now, Ma. I'll talk to you later. Love you, Mel.

P.S.
I'm getting estimates for your gravestone, which will be like Daddy's. As I get more information about this, I will tell you.

October 28, 1996

Dear Ma,
Although I didn't want to make the trip, we went to Barbara and Patty's and stayed all day Saturday. Once the traveling is over, it's nice to see everyone. When we came home, I thought about calling you to let you know we were home, safe and sound. I always did this when you were alive, but this is the first time since your death that I almost called you. I forgot for a second that I couldn't call you. There are no phones in heaven.

I met Saul Mark at the synagogue on Sunday. I had him read your marriage license so we could get your Hebrew name, but we are having a hard time deciphering it. I'll make a copy and send it to the monument people.

The apartment is coming along fine and a lot of work is being done every day. They're placing all the electric, phone and cable lines, and no wires are going to show.

Kay is going for another job interview today. I hope she gets a better job soon. She hates working where she is now.

I received the money from your credit union account and gave Alan and Bert their share. I still have a problem believing that you died. I always look at your photo on the piano and I can see you talking; it's very strange. I keep having dreams about you. It's going to take time for me to accept in my soul that you are gone.

We have to meet the contractor in the apartment tonight to go over a few things with him. Ma, I have to go now; I'll talk to you later. Love, Melville.

October 29, 1996

Dear Ma,

I heard on the radio this morning that Morey Amsterdam died. He was an actor who played a comedy writer on "The Dick Van Dyke Show." He was eighty-five years old. When one reaches the eighties, according to Kay's father, he/she is living on borrowed time. I heard Henny Youngman, at eighty-eight years old, say, "I went to a restaurant and ordered three-minute eggs and they asked me to prepay it." Personally, I agree with my father-in-law. While of course we all know it is possible to make it to one's nineties, how many people really do? Even so, I wish it had happened to you, Ma. I felt you had a few years left. We don't know when we will die, but when we're in our eighties, we know it will happen soon. I remember and I know I'm repeating myself that when I would say, "next year," you would say, "Let's live until next year." You knew what you were saying; you were being realistic.

I was speaking with Othello last night and he asked me if I were able to talk to you, what would I ask you? I said I want to know that you are all right. Are you all right, Ma? I wish you could let me know. Maybe you're better off. I suppose I will find out someday. I'll talk to you more tomorrow. Love, Mel.

October 30, 1996

Dear Ma,

I remember asking you on occasion if you were bored staying in the house and you said no. Somehow you kept yourself busy with things that occupied your whole day. Josie is so terribly bored that I feel sorry for her, but she can't seem to get herself out of the rut. You had your day planned out, so even when you were in the house, which was basically the last few years, you had things to do so you wouldn't get bored. You read the newspaper; you balanced your checkbook; you cooked dinner for us (although I kept telling you not to), and I know you spoke to a few people during the day. You also knitted and did needlepoint. I think what I'm trying to say is that you made a life for yourself, even in the house. You know, it seems a lot of elderly people have trouble doing that. I'm glad that you seemed content while at home. Love, Mel.

October 31, 1996

Dear Ma,

Today I went to the doctor to get a flu shot and have my cholesterol level checked. As I'm still experiencing some MS symptoms, and they aren't getting any better, and because the last neurologist didn't really do much, I've decided to see another neurologist who was recommended by my internist. I can't help but wonder if your death has exacerbated my MS. The pain, weakness, and instability in my left leg still bother me; it's not terrible, but I know it's there.

Ma, will I ever be able to believe that you have died? I don't know, but we'll see what it's like when the years pass by. At this moment, I can still feel your presence.

The flu shot gave me a headache, so I'm not feeling well today. I'll write to you again tomorrow. I should feel better by then. Love, Mel.

November 2, 1996

Dear Ma,

Yesterday was very busy in my office, that's why I didn't get a chance to write to you. I could hear you say, "I'm glad you have more business." I miss having you say things like that to me.

I have to get ready to go back to the synagogue. Alan, Sharon and Susan are coming in tonight to see the apartment. I will only be able to spend a couple of minutes with them because we're going to Kay's cousin's house to have dinner. I'm going to go now, so I'll write to you later. Love, Mel.

November 4, 1996

Dear Ma,

I've been busy. Yesterday I helped Saul Mark clean the yard behind the synagogue. He asked me to help, so I did it. I did Mary Ann a favor and drove her to see her uncle who is in the hospital. When we got home, I wrapped up all the pictures we bought to prepare them for the move to the new apartment. We then went to Josie's for dinner. Kay's sister was there so we brought her up to the apartment to see it. I gave her more lamps, this time the two foyer lamps. I couldn't see throwing them away; they are another reminder that you are gone. She really loves the lamp with the hanging crystals, you know, the one we gave her a couple of months ago. I think she loves it as much as you did. She says when she hears the crystals tinkle, when the wind blows, or when she's cleaning them, she thinks you're talking to her, and of course, she answers

59

you back . . . she says she talks to you all the time. I wonder, do you hear her?

You know, I remember thinking when you were alive, how the apartment needed a paint job. I remember you used to say it was good enough for you. It's funny, when I stop to think, I remember signs of things deteriorating, something that in the past, you would never let happen; for instance, the rusted window sill where you kept the mop, something that I would look at whenever I was in your house. I remember wondering what was going to happen. The house was something like the "portrait of Dorian Gray." I noticed the apartment's deterioration, even if I refused to acknowledge that the same thing was happening to you. Yet on some level, I felt that the end was near, though I really didn't want to think about it, let alone talk about it. I must have been thinking that talking about it might make it happen, God forbid! I miss you, Ma. I'll talk to you tomorrow. Love, Mel.

November 5, 1996

Dear Ma,

We feel it on a subconscious level when someone close to us is about to die, but it's really something we never talk about because it's too painful. It's one of those things that's dealt with when it happens and when it does happen, it's a shock. I seem to be getting through more of the day without thinking about you. Most of the thoughts I have of you are in the hospital, and they are not nice thoughts. I'm looking forward to a time when the only thoughts remaining are the good ones. Somehow, through all the sadness, one does what one needs to do to survive. To do that, I keep working, eating, paying the rent, taking music lessons; in other words, I live. I know you would not want it any other way.

Today is election day. I'm going to leave early because it's quiet in the office and I have a music lesson tonight. I'll speak to you tomorrow. Love, Mel.

November 6, 1996

Dear Ma,

President Clinton was reelected. I think you would be happy.

The thought came into my head, again, of when I walked you down to the operating room. I said to you, "Ma, they're going to give you a new carburetor." I guess I tried to lighten things up by joking, but it didn't work. You didn't seem to appreciate it. This would be the last time you would see me and recognize me as your son. It was a moment I will never forget. I really thought the operation would be a success and that you would be all right. Unfortunately, it did not turn out that way.

I felt the end was coming near, but I guess I just didn't want to believe it. I guess what I'm trying to say is that there was enough evidence that your life was slowing down, and your body was breaking down for me to know you were going to die; I just, of course, didn't know when. Isn't this true for everybody?

I have to go now. I'll talk to you later. By the way, tonight is Alan's retirement party. Love, Mel.

November 7, 1996

Dear Ma,

Alan's retirement party was very enjoyable. There were quite a few people there. Some of the men made speeches and Alan was praised to the hilt. Truth is, everything they said about him was true: hard worker, dedicated to his family (that started when he was young), took on the responsibility of being an adult at a relatively young age. You know, Ma, he is somebody that should be respected. He does a lot of things right and is a fine example of how to be. I hope he can calm down now. Everybody knows he's a little neurotic, including himself! You deserve the credit for the fine person he is, actually, for the way we all are. You not only gave us life, but you taught us how to live. I always told you that, and you should be proud of yourself.

Last night, we were talking about how we all wished you could've been at Alan's retirement party, and Dora started to cry. She loved you like a sister and showed it in many different ways. She's truly a wonderful person. I told her, if she ever needs my help, she could call me anytime.

The house is coming along fine. The contractor is going to order the kitchen and bathroom tile today or tomorrow and Kay and I are going to look at some stained glass we want to put in the kitchen cabinets. As always, I miss talking to you. Love, Mel.

November 11, 1996

Dear Ma,

Sorry I haven't written to you in a few days. Work has been very busy and the weekend never seems to have enough time in it.

The weather seems to be putting me in a melancholy mood. I think about this being the first winter you will not be here. It makes me sad.

Kay and I had dinner with Bert, Gail and Lisa last night. I couldn't help thinking that it was too bad they never had the close relationship with you that Kay and I had. When you were sick, I remember meeting Gail in the hallway of her apartment building and she was crying, telling me how she always had to live with illness. I'm not exactly sure what that meant, but it might've had an impact on how she relates to other people. It's very sad that they missed out on getting to know you well. I don't think they realized how good a person you were.

I went to the synagogue on Saturday. I hope you hear me saying Kaddish. When Jerry came into the synagogue and saw me, he told me that I was doing the right thing; he said most people do not go to the synagogue and say Kaddish, although it is a very important thing to do. Well, I think you deserve it; it's the least I can do.

I have been reading the tax booklets in reference to your estate, gift and trust tax returns. They're a little complicated, but I will get them done. I can see you laughing and saying, "Just look at all these cockamamy tax returns I have to fill out for my farshtinkener fortune!"

Everything else seems to be going okay. I am meeting Kay and Mary Ann tonight for dinner. Because today is Veteran's Day and Kay didn't work, she'll pick me up with the car.

Ma, I love you and I will talk to you tomorrow. Love, Mel.

November 13, 1996

Dear Ma,

Today, I was thinking about how you felt about your grandchildren. You once told me that one can't love a grandchild like a child. I think what you were trying to say was that because a person doesn't get so emotionally involved with grandchildren as she does with her own children, she doesn't love them as she loves her children. Grandchildren do not live with us, so we just don't get that close to them. I know you cared for them and wanted them to be healthy and happy. You always asked about them and were happy when they called you. I remember your telling me that Jason had called you from Granada, and he told you he loved you. You were tickled by that. I know you were pleased when Jarett called you when he came in from school. He didn't always do that, but when he did, you were happy. It's unfortunate that your grandchildren didn't get to know you better. They would've learned an awful lot from you. You were very wise about many things.

The house is coming along. Yesterday they put in the bathtub. Soon they will prime the house and start the painting. It's a project that takes time to do.

Ma, I will always miss you. Love, Mel.

November 15, 1996

Dear Ma,

I had a terrific week in the office. I billed my highest amount ever. I will also get the largest check I ever have. I can't help but think that you have something to do with it. I feel you're always looking down and watching and maybe nudging people to place orders with me who might otherwise not. If you're doing that for me, all I can say is "thank you."

I still have those thoughts about you in the hospital. I think about them every day. Different scenarios go through my head where you come out all right. This is what I dream, but know could never be. I think about you in the grave and it hurts me to envision you like that. I just can't seem to let go of those thoughts. Whenever I think of them, I still want to see a different outcome. I build up a whole story about your getting sick, but then getting better; it's a desire that cannot be fulfilled.

I received your last pension check today. It was for $10.81. That was for August 1, the day you died.

My whole demeanor seems to be one of sadness. My thoughts, as you can tell, are always of you. They are sad thoughts. Every time I go into the apartment I imagine where you would be sitting in the kitchen, or sitting on the bed in the bedroom. I loved you, and your not being here any more is not an easy thing to overcome. Not that I want to stop loving you, but learning to live without you is what has to happen.

I guess we will go up to the house tonight to see what's going on. It's the weekend, so tomorrow I'll go to the synagogue and on Sunday I'll stay home.

Ma, I'll talk to you tomorrow. Love, Mel.

November 18, 1996

Dear Ma,

Bert called me this morning and said to me, "I sit in the living room and look at Mama's photo and can't believe she's gone." I told him I understand this because I feel exactly the same way. Last night, we went to our (and your) favorite Chinese restaurant. It's not the same going there without you. Bert says he thinks about you all the time; so do I. It's hard to put your absence out of my mind. These writings seem to help me express my feelings about what happened. I really can't tell them to anyone in such an extensive way, so expressing them in these letters to you makes me feel better. What I am thinking about today is when you walked out of the bedroom and said, "I hope I see my house again."

I speak to Ben every couple of weeks and he's doing okay. Alan is still enjoying his retirement. You would be proud of him if you were alive.

On Saturday, I went and said Kaddish for you, and on Sunday, I helped Saul in the synagogue. The weekend was otherwise quiet.

Ma, I'll talk to you tomorrow. Love, Mel.

November 19, 1996

Dear Ma,

I keep thinking of the belching you experienced. You kept complaining of the belching and nobody understood what it was. Isn't that the classic sign of a heart problem? Dr. Roth and Dr. Schwartz did not seem to think so. All the things that were happening to you the last few months before you died were indications that something was wrong, but nobody was intelligent enough to figure that out except for you. You said to me, "Something is very wrong," and the doctors could not seem to help you. I don't understand why the doctors didn't ask any questions or delve further into it. I'm angry at myself for not making them do further testing. I should have known something was wrong. Maybe I could have saved your life. The problems you had, such as the rash, where the hell did that come from? The bad case of the runs, why you had that, who knows? You didn't eat anything different from what you usually ate. That restlessness in your feet you were getting all the time. To me, these were all signs of something wrong, and I wasn't smart enough to know. But the doctors, shouldn't they have known? I guess doctors are not as smart as we think they are. They certainly don't know everything!

I'm sorry, Ma, that I was not smart enough to know. I wish that I were. I feel that I'm in despair. Your death has caused me grief and torment. I feel tormented because I felt I should have known something was wrong and maybe could have done something about it. I feel grief because you have died and I miss you.

I felt this exact way when Dad died. I didn't understand it then, and I don't now; except maybe now, because I am a man, I can deal with it on a different level. When I was a boy and Dad died, death was the furthest thing from my mind. As a matter of fact, no one expected Dad to die. He was only fifty-six years old! His death was devastating to me. He was my link to the outside world. He was someone I was very dependent on. He was my identity. It led me on a search to find a trustworthy replacement. Twelve years later, I found Othello. Now, as an adult, I am self-sufficient and more in touch with my feelings, and therefore, I can deal with death on a different level. But it's still part of the unknown and beyond my understanding.

I'm going to go now, Ma. I'll talk to you later. Love, Mel.

November 21, 1996

Dear Ma,

How are you doing? This is what you always used to say when I visited you. I wish that I could ask you that question. The thoughts of you are always the same. A story always runs through my thoughts in which you don't die. Somehow, the operation saves you, or we find out that you are sick early enough to take care of it before you have your heart attack. These are really just dreams and a dream is what we hope for, but hoping is not going to help the situation. Death is so final. There is no way out. The only thing we could hope for is that there is something after death, and, if there is, then I'm sure you can see and hear me. There must be some kind of connection to the spirit world.

I hope someday I get a sign from you. You know, sometimes when I walk or drive past a lamppost (it could be any lamppost, anywhere), the light, if it's on, will suddenly go off, or if off, come on. The question is, are you trying to communicate with me? I always say, "Hi, Ma," or "Hi, Dad," just in case.

Tonight, I'm going to see that neurologist I mentioned before. I'm still having a minor problem with my leg, which I hope we could take care of. Dr. Leeds used to take care of these things all the time. I never told you, but there were a few times over the last twenty-five years when I had recurring MS symptoms, but Dr. Leeds would always prescribe some medication that would take care of them. But now that Dr. Leeds moved to California, I have to find another doctor. I'll keep looking until I find one I have confidence in. This is no easy task, because as you know, Dr. Leeds saved my life.

I'll talk to you tomorrow. Love, Mel.

November 25, 1996

Dear Ma,

On Thursday, the neurologist I saw prescribed the medication that Dr. Leeds used to prescribe for me, called dexamethasone. It can make you feel ill, but I only have to take it for three days. I just hope it works. I'll let you know. This doctor also suggested that I see Dr. Henry, who specializes in helping multiple sclerosis patients.

I was thinking last night what it is that I received, or should I say, what I learned, from everybody in the family. I started with your parents and it went something like this:

From your father, Gershon, I learned what it was to be treated special, because he always bought me presents (e.g., my blue bicycle); from your mother, Sophie, I learned wisdom and how to do business (we'd always fight over the change after she sent me to the drug store because she knew she'd have to get something back, but I didn't want to give it to her); from Dad I learned about art, to see the beauty of it and the feel of it and the appreciation of it, whether it was music, art, film, whatever. From you, Ma, I learned how to be logical. You were always able to apply logic to situations and come up with the answer. You also taught me about survival, by doing just that after Dad died. You taught me the value of a dollar, how to shop and be thrifty, and most of all, how to be a good person, because that's what you were. From my brother Alan I learned responsibility. Just by watching him, even at such a young age, it rubbed off and made me the same way. From my brother Bert I learned salesmanship and how to deal with people on a personal level. He's the best salesman that I know. He also taught me how to laugh. Through thick and thin, he seemed to always come out with a smile.

The person we become is a reflection of the personalities that surround us. I'm so thankful that I was surrounded by good people. I love them all.

Ma, I'll talk to you again tomorrow. Love, Mel.

P.S.
I keep thinking, what if you had the angiogram done sooner? Would it have made a difference? I have to believe it would have because your heart would not have been so badly damaged from the heart attack. The thought keeps running through my mind that we should've known you needed medical help because all kinds of peculiar

things were happening to you in the last month, such as the belching, diarrhea, and the rash you had all over your body.

I keep thinking about this. I guess I am blaming myself and I can't do that. I did not cause you to get sick, and don't know if I could have done anything to save you, yet I still feel frustrated that I couldn't do anything and keep wondering if something could've been done. I'm not going to feel guilty about this anymore. I have to get beyond this. I know that's what you would want.

December 2, 1996

Dear Ma,

Today is the second day in December. I have not written to you for a whole week. It seems that I am running out of things to say. How many times can I say the same thing? It's time to let go of those thoughts that I have about you in the hospital and when you got sick. There is nothing that can be changed about it. All those things that I talked about happened; they are now history. I think you would want me to let them go and resolve them. I seem to be at that stage in the process where realization is setting in. When we suffer a loss, we go through a process until we accept it.

I am now dealing with the MS. Although I am in fairly good shape, things are bothering me. My left side is weaker and I can feel it when I walk, but I push myself to do it. The MRI I had done showed some lesions in the right side of the brain. I know you didn't want to believe it, but I do have MS. On December 12 I have an appointment with Dr. Henry. Supposedly, he is a top MS doctor. I hope so. Anyway, Ma, this is what I have to think about and deal with now.

You know, Ma, when I say I want to stop thinking about you, it's the painful thoughts I want to stop thinking about. You know that I love you. We had a good relationship, and for that, I am grateful. I feel the time is coming when these letters to you will end. We'll see what happens. Ma, I'm going to go now. Love, Mel.

December 5, 1996

Dear Ma,
I think I'm feeling better. I say "think" because sometimes it's hard to tell. I'm trying to put your death in its proper perspective; that is, to remember the good things, not the bad things you went through. I want to make myself feel better again. Like anybody else, I don't like feeling sick. I am hoping that, if I feel better emotionally, I will feel better physically. Just as I suspected, I experienced an exacerbation of the MS after you got sick. I'm hoping that it will go into remission if I get over the sadness and can find joy in the thoughts I have of you. This is one of the reasons I cut back on writing to you. I always wrote about those bad times. It would always make me feel sad and I think this aggravated the MS condition. Therefore, I'm trying to stop myself from thinking about you in the hospital.

I'm going to go now, Ma, it's late. I'll speak to you tomorrow. Love, Mel.

December 6, 1996

Dear Ma,

I wanted to talk to you about Kay. She hates her job. The problem is, she does not like auditing. As I see it, she feels she is not good at auditing and always telling herself that has, I think, made her lose confidence. I get the feeling she thinks she won't be able to handle anything. I think she should stop telling herself she can't do auditing because when one keeps telling herself something, she starts to believe it. So now, if she gets a job in budgeting, she's saying that she doesn't know if she could do it. She's afraid. It's fear of failure. If she found what she would like to do, she would be excellent at it, because, whether she thinks so or not, she has an impact on people and the work that she does, such as her boss saying, "You're the glue." She has some great qualities that everybody sees. Does she see them but think they are not real? Maybe she thinks people are patronizing her. She needs to leave the job she's in now, and to do that, she needs to sit down and think about what she likes and dislikes. She'll be surprised where her thoughts might take her. I wish you could tell me what you thought, Ma. You always had a logical answer.

I'll talk to you later. Love, Mel.

December 13, 1996

Dear Ma,

I haven't written for an entire week for a few reasons. Firstly, I am running out of things to say to you. If you were able to answer me then there would be a conversation. Secondly, I have been busy in the office, and thirdly, I haven't been feeling well. The MS, I told you, has returned. The new doctor I found, Dr. Henry, is dealing with it the same way Dr. Leeds did. He's giving me a powerful dosage of steroids which are making me sick (e.g., heartburn, belching, nausea), but it'll be worth it if they work and control the symptoms. I know, Ma, you didn't want to believe I had MS, but unfortunately, I do. The MRI now proves it. I have to go for another MRI of the spine on Tuesday. I'll let you know what happens.

The apartment renovation is progressing well. We will go up there tonight to see if they put the tile in the bathroom. As you know, all the doors in the apartment, including the two bedrooms, the bathroom and the four closets were hollow; a lot of them were also damaged. The contractor felt it was high time they were replaced with solid doors, and this was supposed to happen today.

Alan and Bert are doing okay. Kay is also okay. I received the bill for the gravestone and am going to mail out a check today. I think you would be pleased with the gravestone and the bed of stones. It was done exactly as you requested and is an exact duplicate of Daddy's.

Time is passing by. You have been gone four and one-half months and it just doesn't seem possible. Those bad thoughts and feelings have taken a back seat to the MS I now have to deal with. I think I'll be all right, though I must admit that I am a little worried. I have to be on the medication that Dr. Henry gave me for twenty days, and when it's finished I will see him again.

I miss talking to you about things, but Ma, I can't seem to write to you anymore. These conversations to you are descriptions of my feelings. The whole premise about them, I think, is false. My feelings are true, but a conversation? No, it's not. That is what is false. It's not even a letter. It's more like a diary. Tomorrow I will go to the synagogue to say Kaddish, as usual. You must be looking down on me and showering me with your tender loving care, because I feel enveloped by your spirit; I feel safe. You and Dad always made me feel safe.

Ma, I will talk to you next week again. I miss you. Love, Mel.

December 16, 1996

Dear Ma,

I've been taking the medicine now for four days, and feeling sick and out of sorts, but because I've experienced this before, I know I'll survive this episode. Tomorrow I go for an MRI of the spine to see if any spinal disease has developed. Dr. Henry said that might be a possibility. I'm not sure I know what that means, but we will find out when I go back to see him.

I went up to the apartment tonight by myself. Kay stayed home to do homework. I walked around and looked and reminisced about the things that happened. I was standing in front of the back bedroom door and was staring at the side of the bed Dad was on the night he died. I was going into the bathroom when he looked at me in despair, holding his chest and shaking his head. That was the last time I saw him alive. I think now about it and it seemed that he was saying good-bye with his eyes. Then I walked into your bedroom and remembered your sitting on the bed getting ready to go to the hospital. You were frightened but knew you had to go; then, in the living room, thinking about Baba, when she slept in there; then in the kitchen, imagining where you used to sit at the kitchen table. There are good spirits running around the house. I hope they are always there and expect they will be. I'm positive that all of you are watching over us. I love you all, Mel.

December 22, 1996

Dear Ma,

I haven't written for over a week because I'm feeling sick from the steroids. I have another nine days to go on them, but at least I took the heavier dosages in the beginning. The dosage will start decreasing now. I just hope the medicine works, but it's still too early to tell.

Every time I pass the light pole downstairs, it goes on! I always have the feeling you and Dad are talking to me, telling me that everything will be okay. I hope you're watching out for me.

I know I've slowed down on the writing. Well, for one thing, the MS has taken the forefront right now. For another thing, I realize that no matter how much I say, or think, or do, I reached a point in the mourning process where I have to move on with my life. In essence, if I can't, then really, two people die, not to mention all the people who are around me that are affected by it. So that's the stage I'm at, just trying to move on, and now working through the MS difficulty. In a few days it will be 1997, another new year, another new beginning. Although there were some bright spots and happy times in 1996, I'm sure, for the rest of my life, I will remember it as a sad year. I hope you are resting in peace wherever you may be.

Thinking about you now, all I can say is, I thank you for the life you gave me, for everything that you taught me, for the love that you gave me, and for being so wise. I thank you for making me the person that I am today. I am a good person and I owe it to you and Dad. I realize that I am the culmination of your bodies, your teachings, your thoughts, your goodness, your very essence. I hope I keep living up to these ideals and make you proud. Love, Mel.

December 29, 1996

Dear Ma,

I have been feeling miserable. The medicine has made me feel weak at times. I'm taking a huge dosage of powerful steroids, and they make me quite ill. Yesterday I felt better, but today I feel worse. I don't know how I will feel tomorrow. Presently, I have no control over all the sensations that are going through me. I can't wait to be finished with the steroids. I want to feel better. I lost sixteen pounds in sixteen days. I'm not happy about that, but I'm just trying to get through it, and Wednesday is the last day I take the medicine. Thursday I have an appointment to see Dr. Henry.

We just met Alan and Sharon and went up to the apartment. Alan thinks it looks like a different apartment and I think if you saw it, you would love it.

Ma, I know you are looking down on us and smiling, because as you can see, we have all remained friends, which was the most important thing to you.

I haven't much more to say right now. I love you and will speak to you later. Love, Mel.

January 1, 1997

Dear Ma,

You died five months ago. It seems like yesterday. Time seems to fly by.

January 5, 1997

Dear Ma,

It's 1997. We went up to Lorraine and Vito's for New Year's Eve. Kay's parents were there and you would have been there also. I will always consider 1996 a painful year. First, your death in August, then the MS exacerbation, and then the cure (which made me so sick, I thought it was worse than the "disease"). It's going to take a couple of weeks for the medicine to work its way out of my body.

But looking on the brighter side of things, the apartment is coming along; the painting is done, they are getting ready to tile the floors, and we should be able to move in next month. It will be a good beginning for a new year.

Alan's enjoying his retirement. He says he doesn't miss work, not one bit. Every time he calls and leaves a message on the answering machine, he says, "Hi, this is the recent retiree calling . . . " He is keeping himself busy doing things he has never done before. Sharon leaves him lists, which include things such as shopping, vacuuming, and going to the cleaners. He also takes Sharon to the railroad station in the morning and picks her up in the evening. He's decided to try and find a part-time job.

I'm going to give Alan and Bert their share of the apartment, although when we discussed it, you told me the

78

apartment was mine. I told you that if Alan and Bert didn't get their fair share it would make for bad feelings, so I will definitely give them their share.   I cleaned out your apartment and I have also been working on the myriad tax forms required to settle the estate, and being a novice, it has been a herculean effort.   But if I didn't do it myself, I would've had to pay attorneys fees, which I didn't want to do. And Ma, knowing you, you would definitely agree.

Anyway, because I haven't been feeling so good, I haven't gone to Shul the last couple of Saturdays, but I will try to go next Saturday. Dr. Henry said people feel better once they stop taking the medicine, so I'm looking forward to that time.

That's all I have to say today. I will speak to you soon. Love, Mel.

January 13, 1997

Dear Ma,

I am depressed today. I am thinking about you. Saturday was your birthday. You would have been eighty-four years old. I'm sorry you didn't make it to this day. Those thoughts of you in the hospital have crept back into my consciousness again.   I guess that will happen from time to time. How stupid I was to tell you they were going to put a new carburetor in you. That was the last thing I ever said to you. How dumb! I guess I just didn't know what to say. When those thoughts come back, the hurt comes back, also.

We'll be moving into your apartment soon. Moving is one of the worst things I have had to do in my life. Having to look at every item I own, from a holey college sweatshirt, that I've kept for sentimental reasons, to my last bit of scrap paper, and decide what I want to take, is a huge, tedious job. We are only moving down the street, but the work is necessary just the same. In fact, it seems worse because we are only going a short distance.

The cold weather, coupled with the MS (which, finally, has gotten somewhat better) and the pressure of moving, has gotten me down. I don't like feeling this way and I can't wait until we are on the Caribbean cruise. When we get to that point, everything will be behind us. I guess there will come a time when I will look back at this period and say it was quite an experience.

Knowing your birthday was Saturday has gotten me down. Thinking about you dying has gotten me down. Bert called me today and told me Jane Unger (our next-door neighbor) died. And also, Frank's wife (who lived downstairs) died. All the original people that lived in these buildings are passing away, but time keeps marching on and another generation follows. Then they will die, and the next generation moves into their spot, and so on and so forth. Time does not stop. I'm not sure I know what I'm trying to say, Ma, but I'll speak to you later. Love, Mel.

January 16, 1997

Dear Ma,
    Bad news. Janet has lung cancer. I hope you can look down on her and help her. It was diagnosed Wednesday. Tomorrow and next Tuesday she goes for more tests. I hope they can help her and, if you can, put in a good word for her. I know I didn't really have to ask you that.

Anyway, I'm feeling better. On January 30 I have an appointment with Dr. Henry. I don't know if he will give me more medicine or not. We'll see. I would rather not take it.

The apartment is almost finished. We will likely move in on Sunday, February 2. The kitchen cabinets are coming next Thursday and everything else is almost finished. This weekend we will move pictures over. I will speak to you again soon. Nothing more to say right now. Love, Mel.

January 20, 1997

Dear Ma,

Janet got a bit of good news. The cancer did not spread to her bone marrow. Next Thursday they perform a scan on the rest of her body. I hope she's okay. Dora is having a tough time with it, as any parent would. I hope she is okay, too.

We moved a ton of stuff over to your apartment this weekend, all the stuff we were physically able to carry, such as all the cartons, the pictures, the clothes, etc. Mary Ann and Kay's parents helped us. It took a lot of trips, but we did it. Kay, Mary Ann and I are sore from the lifting and carrying. The only thing left to move is the furniture. I wonder what you would say if you saw the apartment. I know you would be happy for us. We think it's beautiful. I wish you were here to see it.

I'm still going to Shul on Saturdays to say Kaddish for you, which I know you would appreciate. I miss you. I will talk to you later. Love, Mel.

January 31, 1997

Dear Ma,

The movers will be moving the furniture this weekend. I hope you are with us and are happy for us. I know you wanted me to have the apartment, but I can't help wondering what you would think about all the changes we made. I think you would like what we have done, but the cost of doing it would appall you. I could hear you saying, "What are you, CRAZY!?"

I think about you often. I think about the time we sat on the bench together, not too long before we went to Alaska. You were looking at an elderly man who lives in our apartment complex, and you were saying how wonderfully the home-care worker was taking care of him. I think you were putting yourself in his place, and hoping that if you ever got to that point, that you would be taken care of in the same manner. Sometimes when I say Kaddish, I think of us sitting there.

I have ambivalent feelings about moving in to the apartment. On the one hand, I feel it's still your apartment and I'm trespassing, but then I know you're gone, and you wanted me to be there. I really haven't had time to dwell on these feelings because of everything that has been going on, including the move, the MS, work, and the dreary winter. The time has come, and we have a lot to do, so I will speak to you later. Love, Mel.

February 5, 1997

Dear Ma,

Today is my birthday, as if you didn't know. It's unfortunate that you are not here with us to celebrate it. Not that I'm going out on the town, but I do wish you were here.

I'm forty-five years old today, but I don't feel like I'm forty-five. The years have passed by quickly. I would have to say that although Dad died in 1964, it seems like only yesterday. That's not to say if Dad didn't die, it would not have seemed that way. But today is my birthday, I feel good, the MS seems to be under control, I'm working and making a decent wage, and my life is okay right now.

We moved in all our furniture over the weekend. Bert helped me reassemble the bed and install the air conditioners. The apartment looks beautiful and I think we'll be very happy here. This is my family's apartment and everybody who lived in it has, and always will, make me happy.

I got a notice for Yartzeit for Daddy. It will be in a couple of weeks.

At forty-five years old, I have experienced a lot of things in my life, both good and bad. I experienced death, illness, divorce, loss of a business and felt the pain of all of it. I'm thankful none of these things has made me bitter. I still laugh, smile and am generally in good spirits. I could've been a comedian. Fear stops us from doing things. I think lack of confidence also holds us back. But, I hope, with maturity, and by working at it, I can learn how

83

to get over these emotional hang-ups. I'm still trying. I have nothing more to say right now. Love, Mel.

February 13, 1997

Dear Ma,

On Sunday, Kay and I are finally going on the Caribbean cruise for a week with Alan and Sharon. It will be great to be on vacation.

The apartment is 99% finished. By the time we come back from vacation we should be able to move. Then, it's just a matter of finishing the unpacking, putting things away and hanging the pictures.

I think about you so often that I can almost hear you talking to me. As I said the last time I wrote, I miss you. I try to remember just the good times, but some memories always pop up about the way I sometimes treated you, which wasn't always very nice. I sometimes gave you a hard time, and I really shouldn't have. I feel guilty about that, and am sorry that I treated you that way. But in truth, every parent-child relationship—I guess every human relationship—no matter how wonderful, has some rocky moments. But when one of those people dies, the other one is left alone with those thoughts that are hard to resolve, although, in the long run, they are insignificant. Therefore, I try to remember just the good times. Love, Mel.

February 14, 1997

Dear Ma,

Happy Valentine's Day, Ma! Kay and I will be leaving Sunday on our cruise. I will not be writing to you any more till I get back. I keep thinking of last February when we were vacationing in the Cayman Islands, and you surprised me with a telephone call. Although I had given you the phone number of the condo we were staying in, I never expected you to call. I remember when I heard your voice the first thing I said was, "Hi Ma, what's the matter? Are you okay?" But you said everything was fine, you just wanted to know how we were doing. That's what I would like to know about you. How are you doing? That's the thing about death that I don't know and can't find out: how are you doing? Are you okay? That's what I'd like to think. I hope you're doing okay with Dad. He's been wherever it is you are for thirty-three years! That's a long time, time that you should have spent together, but lost. That's the tragedy.

I love you both and miss you both, and will talk to you next week when I get back. Love, Mel.

February 24, 1997

Dear Ma,

Is life but a dream? Dad died on this day, thirty-three years ago.

February 28, 1997

Dear Ma,

Life goes by so incredibly fast that you sometimes wonder where it went to. We have all heard the expression, "You only live once, so enjoy it while you can." Well, there is a lot of truth to that. If in your life, you have not done what you wanted to do, then you are probably living the way someone else wants you to, and your life is just a dream (someone else's dream at that). It's nice to dream. It's also important. It makes you feel good, so imagine how you would feel if you live your own dream and you're in touch with yourself. It seems to me you can live your entire life and be unhappy because you never tried to fulfill your dreams. It's like being in two places at the same time. On one level you're living and doing everything you need to survive, and at the same time you want a completely different life. A dream, like life, goes by very fast. Well, then, if life goes by that fast, to feel good you better live your dream and make it happen.

I wonder sometimes if you did. I know you told me you were happy you had children, and worked, and accomplished something economically, but you told me if you had to do it over again, you wouldn't have married Dad. That was because of his family. Those years were very rough financially and emotionally for you. Aunt Lilly made it hard for you.

Ma, you were always so logical, did you live your life the way you wanted to? Did you feel complete or satisfied when you died? Does a person have to? I know you didn't want to die, so you must have loved life.

Thinking about Dad, I think the only happiness he really had was you. I think your relationship got better after he calmed down. It's too bad that he died so young. Look how much he missed. I wonder, did he live his dream?

We're moving into the apartment tomorrow, Ma. I miss you. Love, Mel.

March 6, 1997

Dear Ma,

Mary Ann's sister, Lorraine, died on March 1. She was forty-four years old, a young woman who had many years to live, but, tragically, she didn't. She was sick for a very long time, and I think she just gave up. Mary Ann, like me, is feeling so alone. She has also lost both her parents, and now, her only sister. I know that she can always count on her brother-in-law, Vito, and his family, and I want her to know that she will always have us as family, too.

I spoke to Jarett today and it was good to hear from him. I understand now his feelings toward Bert. He is angry. I think he feels Bert abandoned him and he has trouble understanding why. Why did Bert stop taking him on Sundays? How do you explain to a child, or the man who was the child, the effects of a bitter divorce resulting from a destructive relationship? These are two nice people that became victims of circumstance, and who is to judge what is right and what is wrong? But what is done is done. Any mistakes that were made, cannot be undone. And we know, Ma, how short life is. I hope they can learn to forgive and forget, and maybe if they can talk about the feelings they had in those trying times, they can build a better relationship.

After moving into the apartment we found a few things that needed to be fixed. The contractor was supposed to be in this week to fix them, but he didn't make it. Eventually, he will get there.

I'll talk to you tomorrow. Love, Mel.

March 18, 1997

Dear Ma,

Kay and I still have a lot of work to do cleaning up and hanging pictures. This is happening in the middle of tax season. Happily, we don't have too many tax returns to complete.

I haven't been feeling well. My arms itch and my legs hurt. I just called Alan and he said everybody and everything is fine. I think of you often. We have your photo in your old bedroom, now our den (we refer to it as the "yellow bedroom"). I always look at it, thinking that you're talking to me. Time seems to go by so fast. I keep feeling that life is like a dream. It seems that you died only yesterday. But it wasn't yesterday, it was eight months ago. It takes a long time to feel settled again. Thinking about it, I don't know if I'll ever feel settled. When one goes through a traumatic experience, it shocks him, and when in shock it takes time to get back to normal. But just because a part of me is on pause, life doesn't stop. The world keeps spinning on its axis, time keeps forging ahead, and things keep happening.

I recently had a recurrence of weakness from the MS that lasted several months. I'm still bothered with it, but I can't complain too much — I'm happy I'm not crippled, because that's what might have happened. Then we contracted to have the apartment redone, which has been going on since November. Then, we went on a cruise . . . where did that week go? We moved from one apartment to another, living with Kay's parents in between. Life seems a little upside down now, but life goes on, and time goes on.

I hope I stay healthy enough to pay back the debt on the apartment. Kay hopes so, too! I think you went through that topsy-turvy feeling, Ma, when Dad died. Your life changed after that. We'll talk more tomorrow. Love, Mel.

March 25, 1997

Dear Ma,

Othello was here yesterday. I could hear you saying, Ma, "You're not cured yet?!" The answer is yes, I am, but it's really not a matter of being cured or not. We go to therapy to learn a new way to think. Anyway, we talk about life. I keep asking, is life but a dream? I talked about this a couple of days ago. When a person dreams, it's usually of happy things, or of things that make him or her feel good. The question is, how do we turn dreams into reality? Life is what we make of it and therefore we should be able to take our dreams and make them reality. Of course, all dreams cannot be reality, or to put it another way, all life cannot be a dream. My life, now, is definitely not a dream. I don't feel well, I'm not settled in the apartment, I had an episode while taking medicine, and you died last August. These things are real, not things that I dream about. When we're happy and everything is great we could say life is a dream. So how do we do this? Firstly, we have to think about what we want. What kind of life are we wishing for? Once we know and understand what it is we want, then we have to sit down and do some planning about how to get there. We must not let any fear get in the way. We have to step into the fear to get past it. The most important thing is to think about what we want to do and how to get there. If we do this, we'll come up with a way to make our dreams reality. Again, before we can do this, we must know what the dream is. What is it that we want? What is it that will make us happy? Ma, am I making sense? I know I can hear you say, "So who's happy today?"

I find myself looking at the art in the house and escaping into the pictures.

I have to go now. Love, Mel.

April 8, 1997

Dear Ma,

I would love to be able to ask you the question, "How are you?" and get an answer, but obviously, I can't. You know, I go around the apartment and am overwhelmed with memories of things that have happened, both good and bad. I have memories of when we first moved in and the apartment was empty. I remember Dad doing some work in the living room. I remember Dad sitting in the foyer smoking his cigar while watching TV, and I would put my ear on top of his head. I remember we had a parakeet, Chip, and it would fly and land on his head. When Dad would drink beer, the bird would get on the edge of the glass for a drink. Dad would tip the glass so the bird could get some beer and he really got a kick out of that. I remember watching the New York Mets baseball games with Dad and he would get irritated because Casey Stengel did something he didn't like.

I stand in the kitchen and think about when I was maybe seven or eight years old, and one time I touched the refrigerator handle and the worktable countertop and got an electric shock. I couldn't let go until you pulled me off. I remember hearing Dad go to work in the morning. I remember your going to work in the morning, Ma, except, you stopped to wake me up to go to school. I hated that.

When I lay down to go to bed at night, I think of Dad, and when he died in the bedroom, looking at him, so helpless lying in bed, with his hand on his chest. I think about you, Ma, sitting on the bed, in the now-yellow bedroom, which was your room, and telling you we better go to the hospital. I'm talking about the night Kay and I got home from Alaska. I think about how you and Baba used to fight. Then she would get mad and sit in the living room in the dark.

I remember fighting with Alan and Bert in the bedroom, and one time we broke open a pillow and the feathers got all over the place. I remember Alan typing every night on his Facet typewriter. How all three of us lived in that bedroom, I'll never know. My nieces and nephews don't know how good they have it. I remember sitting shivah for Dad after he died. My whole being is wrapped up in this apartment. Although we had construction done to change the shape of the apartment, to me, the apartment is still the same. I love the good memories and the feeling I have from them. By living in the apartment, I feel embraced by all of it. I think about you and Dad moving in when you were in your forties, which is how old Kay and I are now. It's strange to think of that.

I just keep wondering what it would be like if you and Dad were alive today. We would have had a great relationship, but you left me with wonderful memories and feelings of love.

I'm going to go now. I love you both, Mel.

April 17, 1997

Dear Ma,

I've been thinking about you and Dad today. . . . I remember seeing Dad staring out the kitchen window the night he died. I remember the look on his face; it wasn't a look of fright, like you had when you went into the operating room; it was a look of worry. Living in the apartment, I constantly think of you both and wonder where all the time has gone. The years just seem to fly by with each passing moment. I miss you both, but I'm glad to be in your presence in the apartment. I can feel you both here.

I hope business keeps up. So far, it's been quite good. I'd like to pay for the apartment renovation and get out of debt, and, because time zooms by, it will be paid for before we know it.

The apartment is slowly getting straightened out. As I said, it takes time, but eventually we will get it the way we want it

I'm going to go now. It's time to go home. Love, Mel.

April 21, 1997

Dear Ma,

Today is the first night of Passover. It's strange not having Passover with you, Ma. Because you're not here to prepare for the holiday, we are really not having one. Alan and Sharon went to Florida. Bert and Gail stayed home and Kay and I stayed home. I guess we're just not ready to celebrate the holiday without you.

Anyway, Mary Ann and Kay made your chicken soup recipe the other day. It came out well, but I think because we didn't use a kosher chicken, it didn't taste the same as yours. It didn't look the same, either. Next time, we'll buy a kosher chicken. Also, do you remember that I mentioned that I gave my friend Alice Meyer the largest pot you had? Well, she told me she really loves this pot, and to show her appreciation she gave us a sample of the stuffed cabbage she made in it. She also said she plans to give us samples every holiday, whenever she makes it. I told her it isn't necessary, but I must admit it tastes great!

I'm trying to think of something I wanted to write today, but I can't remember what it is. I thought about it in the middle of the night. It was something I did as a child and now I can't remember what it is. I hate when that happens. I guess it will come back to me at some point. I miss not experiencing the holiday. Passover was always a time of the family getting together and learning the history of our people.

I have to leave now. I'll talk to you tomorrow. Love, Mel.

April 24, 1997

Dear Ma,

When I was married to Ann, we lived in Brooklyn, and there wasn't any feeling of a holiday in that particular neighborhood. Now that I'm back in your apartment, I'm remembering past holidays. When you and Dad were alive, the holiday had more significance for me. Everybody was living at home and there was more participation. I remember Dad hiding the matzoh on top of your bedroom door and we never found it. When it was just you, Ma, you made the holiday important and it felt good. Not being with you and Dad has made me depressed. I must say, I keep wondering where you are. I keep going to the synagogue, but it's strained because, sad to say, we barely make a minyan. There has got to be something more to it. The religious are so involved with the religion that it seems to direct their lives completely. It takes a great deal of effort to be religious. These people should be proud of themselves, but they shouldn't judge anybody else. Love, Mel.

May 2, 1997

Dear Ma,

I miss you. I feel a great void in my life. I feel the emptiness. When you were alive, Ma, although Dad was not around, I never felt a void like this. You were always there to fill it. But now, I don't have either of you and it doesn't feel good. Love, Mel.

May 9, 1997

Dear Ma,

Work is getting boring, but because I am a responsible person, I do what I have to do. But there is something missing. It's difficult to find work that we love to do. Of course, the first thing we have to do is find out what our interests and strengths are. I suppose I should have done something in the arts, because that's where my interest lies, such as playing the guitar, for instance. I definitely got this from Dad; after all, he was a musician. I still have his violin and keep thinking that some day I'd like to learn how to play it. I can't help but wonder how my life would have turned out if I had made music my career, instead of my hobby. The things we love are what we do best.

This Sunday is Mother's Day. We went to visit your grave last week, Ma, Alan, Bert, Sharon, Kay and I. It was very nice that all of us came together. I hope you were able to see that everything was fine.

Ma, I'm going to go now. I'll talk to you next week. Love, Mel.

May 15, 1997

Dear Ma,

If you can help Janet, now is the time. The lung cancer has spread to the inside of her lung. She's having a lot of trouble breathing. They are supposed to start a different chemotherapy treatment. I hope it works. It makes me think again how life is but a dream, so short, no matter how many years we live. In the span of time, it's a blink of an eye. I always think about you and how it would be if both

95

you and Dad were here today. At least, Ma, I was with you in the later stages of your life. Dad just died too soon.

It's late, and I'm in the office, so I'm going to leave. Love, Mel.

May 28, 1997

Dear Ma,
How's your spirit? I hope it's at peace. You know, Ma, I keep thinking if I had only taken you to another doctor. I seem to always think about this. I know I have written about it before, but I just always think of you being saved. It's what I wish for but can never have.

Your apartment is almost completely finished. Bob has to come in and finish putting the molding in the last few spots around the kitchen floor. The apartment is beautiful and I'm sure if you saw it, you would think so, too. I hope that your spirit roams around the apartment, blessing things. I can't help but think that you are around. I wonder how Dad's spirit is. Is he at peace? He seemed to have been in pain when he was alive. I think he felt betrayed by his sisters. No, that's the wrong word . . . I should say disappointed. I hope he was able to put his anger aside and find peace. It would be a good thing to know he has.

Our cooperative is finished reconstituting. Now Mary Ann will be able to buy our old apartment so I will be able to pay Alan and Bert for their share of your apartment.

I still feel as though something is missing in my life. It's not a good feeling; it's a painful one. It's amazing how easily this feeling can be brought back to life, just by thinking about that loved one's not being here. I'll talk to you soon. Love, Mel.

June 3, 1997

Dear Ma,
   Another day in my life has gone by.

June 12, 1997

Dear Ma,
   I don't know what to say any more about your death. Death is so final. That's the scary part about it, our not seeing or talking to each other anymore. I am at the point where I must accept it. I hope that you are looking down, that your spirit is real. In the dictionary, death is "a permanent cessation of all vital functions: the end of life." It's the "permanent" aspect I have to get used to. Love, Mel.

July 18, 1997

Dear Ma,
   You died almost one year ago. Just before you died, when we were on the cruise in Alaska, I remember speaking to you and getting the feeling something was wrong. You wanted to tell me, but didn't, because I was on vacation and I wasn't smart enough to pursue it. The same day we got home from vacation, when Kay called you on the phone to tell you we were home, I remember she told me that you didn't sound right and she thought we should go visit you. Well, we went right up to your house and

Bert showed up a couple of minutes after we did. When Bert saw you he immediately knew something was wrong. He said to me, "Mel, we have to take Mama to the hospital" and you agreed. That's when I knew something was terribly wrong. Two weeks later, you were gone.

Thinking back, it made me feel that you were waiting for me to get home. To me, it seemed like a supernatural event and further evidence of your love for me. I miss you. After all, you were the one constant in my life. We went through a lot together. I saw you do some wonderful things and because of all this, I miss you. I miss Dad, also, but because I was so young when he died, the effect was completely different. His dying so long ago shaped my life. Your dying now gives me a completely different perspective. I'm sort of on the other end of the telescope. At twelve, I was looking at the next thirty-three years to come; now, at forty-five, I'm looking at the thirty-three years that have passed . . . very quickly, I might add.

August 19, 1997

Dear Ma,

In the Jewish calendar, today is the anniversary of your death. It's probably the reason I've been feeling a little down. I've been feeling this way since the cruise, which was the first week in August. If you recall, you were supposed to be on this cruise to Bermuda with us. All the people that were ready to go did come. We had a large party: Alan and Sharon, Lenny and Michele, Mary Ann and Lorraine, Josie and Bob, Kay and I, Dora and Johanna, and one of Johanna's friends, Annette, also came with us. We all had a good time and talked about you often. You also would have enjoyed yourself.

Since I've been home, I haven't wanted to do much of anything. I've been going to work, but I have not really felt like working. I can't seem to get motivated. I'm bored with this job. Don't worry, Ma, I'm not leaving. I think, though, things should be a little different in terms of where I am with my career. This has gotten me down. But it's you, too, Ma. Every time I look at your photo, it just makes me sad. I just go through all the thoughts and dreams again of your getting sick, but always getting better. Time is the only thing that can make me feel better. Love, Mel.

August 25, 1997

Dear Ma,

I had another dream about you. I went to the morgue to see you and the man who was in charge came and opened this heavy door, which was the entrance to a medium-sized room. You were lying in bed, covered with a sheet, and your feet started to move. You then sat up and started talking to me in gibberish. The things you were saying were incomprehensible. The next thing, I found myself back out in the hall, speaking with two men. One was smoking a cigarette and they were telling me it's normal for this to happen after a person dies. The next thing, I saw you sitting on a bus and it started to drive away. I don't know what all this means, if anything. All I know is that you are on my mind. The recurring theme in all these dreams is that you are always alive, yet incommunicado or leaving me.

This past weekend, we went out to Alan's new place in West Hampton Beach. We were all there: Bert, Gail, Lisa,

Mary Ann, Kay and I. I saw Janet, Dora and Susan. We had a fun time. We missed you. Love, Mel.

Thursday, September 4, 1997 1:15 p.m.

Dear Ma,

I met Saul Mark on the bus this morning on my way to the office. He told me he was in the hospital a couple of weeks ago, and had some surgery. He's feeling better, thank God, but it's what he said to me, "My wife and I are falling apart!" that really struck a chord! I told Saul you used to say the very same thing, "I'm falling apart!" I told him how you sarcastically said when you were struggling along, "These are the Golden Years!"

It's tough having to watch a person deteriorate when there's nothing we can do about it, except make that person's life as comfortable as we can. Is this what we live for? If only one could reach this age and be healthy. Oh, well, maybe as science progresses this can be assured. Love, Mel.

September 29, 1997 9:30 a.m.

Dear Ma,

Many things have been happening at this point in time. Alan is having an angiogram done today. Last week, he had a stress test and they found a blockage. Janet is not doing very well either. The cancer, the treatment, all that she has gone through, has taken its toll. It's in God's hands now. Dora is an emotional wreck. Sharon was crying on the phone the other day. The whole situation stinks.

September 29, 1997 3:15 p.m.

Dear Ma,

Janet's kidneys are failing. Alan needs a triple bypass. Sharon said he aged twenty years when the doctor told him. When it rains, it pours. All the feelings of despair that I had when you were sick just came back. It's as if they were right there waiting to return. Mom, life is so fragile. This episode with Janet also shows me how short life really is. Time, as I discussed many times in my conversations with you, goes by in the blink of an eye. We make plans, and God laughs . . . that's the saying of the day. We have no control over our lives. Love, Mel.

September 30, 1997 5:20 p.m.

Dear Ma,

Janet died today at the age of forty-five. She succumbed to the lung cancer. Her body just couldn't fight anymore. Ma, you used to say to me, "this farshtinkener life." God, were you right! Do we ever enjoy our lives? I guess there are moments in time when we do. But that's it . . . it's only moments. Janet is now at peace: no more treatments, no more chemotherapy, no more probing, no more coughing. She doesn't have to struggle for air anymore. I hope she's in a better place. After what she has gone through, it's better for her. I wish her to rest in peace and for her family to have no more sorrow. I know, Ma, if you were alive, you would feel the same.

Ma, remember how I said that your waiting for me to get home seemed like a supernatural event? Well, here's another one that's rather spooky: You know that Mary Ann and Lorraine are sisters, and Sharon and Janet are sisters;

well, Mary Ann and Janet are born on the same day in the same month, and Lorraine and Sharon are born on the same day in the same month; Mary Ann and Sharon are born in the same year and Janet and Lorraine are born in the same year; Janet and Lorraine died in the same year. What does this mean, if anything? Love, Mel.

October 27, 1997

Dear Ma,

Alan underwent heart surgery on Wednesday, October 22. Everything seemed to go okay. It's funny, although you died more than one year ago, I wanted to call you and tell you that Alan was out of surgery. I was nervous and wanted to let somebody know, but obviously I couldn't tell you. Anyway, Alan suffered a minor stroke. When I spoke to him on Thursday, I didn't even understand what he said. His speech was terribly slurred. The doctors don't seem too concerned about it. They said everything should come back to normal. When Kay and I saw him on Monday, his speech was much better. We were able to understand him. He also said that he was feeling better. It's going to take time before he's completely back to normal. When we were there on Saturday, he kept telling us to go home; that was déjà vu. Every time Kay and I were with you, you would always tell that to us.

Always thinking of you. Love, Mel.

EPILOGUE

Going back and reading all these letters that I wrote, I realize that they comprise a synopsis or snapshot of my life with the support of my loved ones. I don't think it's been anything unusual. Many families have gone through the same scenarios and experiences. They have suffered the pain and sorrow of death, the joy of life, the happiness of success and the disappointment of failure. In these letters to my mother, I think I have talked about all these experiences and how they affected my life. Needless to say, the person I am today is based on these experiences. My mother's death, which inspired most of these letters, was another formative experience I went through. I said numerous times how much I love her and miss her. Mom, I'm proud of you and am not ashamed to say it. I'm glad I had you for as long as I did. As for my father, his death is the event that changed my life. It shaped my life in subtle ways. I know I am a good person because of them, and would not have wanted to be raised by anybody else. I am also grateful for the large network of loved ones that I am surrounded with: my wife, brothers, in-laws, uncles, aunts, nieces, nephews, cousins, and friends. Love gets us through. I love you, Mom and Dad. Mel.

ABOUT THE AUTHOR

Melville Gary Finkelstein grew up in the ethnically rich area of the Lower East Side of Manhattan, New York City, where he still lives with his wife. In 1996, after his mother passed away, his need to somehow communicate with her took the form of the written word and chronicles his thoughts, feelings and experiences during her last days and beyond. He is currently in sales, and was previously employed as an accountant. He is presently working on a sequel about his father.

www.ingramcontent.com/pod-product-compliance
Lightning Source LLC
Chambersburg PA
CBHW020542290526
45786CB00002B/999